Author's Note

The present work, coinciding with the fourth centenary of the martyrdom of the Pearl of York, is to a large extent a second edition of *Margaret Clitherow* (1966), which I wrote under the pen-name, 'Mary Claridge'. That book was mostly based upon printed sources, though it contained also the results of some research among documents to which I had been directed by two historians of recusant history.

Since that date I have had opportunities for much further original research, upon which the new portions (slightly more than half) of this book are based. I can only, however, consider it a progress report, for the vast accumulations of archives in York are likely to contain further valuable information relevant to Saint Margaret's life. I have, fortunately, been able to correct a few misstatements in the previous work; for example, she married at the age of eighteen, not fifteen, years, so was more mature at the time of her conversion that I had supposed, and the actual charge upon which she was indicted has been discovered. An unexpected bonus has been the tracing of a link with an eighteenth-century poet who also possessed a sharp and ready wit.

To the acknowledgements in my first edition I have to add the Rev. Alberic Stacpoole, O.S.B., M.C., M.A., formerly editor of the *Ampleforth Journal*, for the loan of books, and for his unfailing encouragement, appreciation and willingness to publish my articles; David M. Palliser, M.A., D.Phil., now G. F. Grant Professor of History in the University of Hull, for allowing me to consult his thesis: '*Some Aspects of the Social and Economic History of York in the Sixteenth Century*' (University of Oxford, 1968); also His Honour Judge Philip C. S. Kershaw, Dr. M. Claire Cross of York University and Mr. Douglas Price, Fellow of Keble College, Oxford, for correcting errors in my previous published work. Any further errors of fact or of interpretation are, of course, my own.

Katharine M. Longley
Hull, November 1985

Contents

		Page
	Preliminary	viii
I	Family Background	1
II	Childhood	7
III	Adolescence — I	19
IV	Adolescence — II	25
V	Marriage	33
VI	Conversion	43
VII	Imprisonment	57
VIII	The Holy Sacrifice	67
IX	The Martyred Priests	75
X	Growth Towards Sanctity	85
XI	Approaching the Climax	103
XII	Arrest	113
XIII	Arraignment	121
XIV	The Last Battles	139
XV	Martyrdom	153
XVI	Comment	161
XVII	Aftermath	167
	Abbreviations	175
	Documentation	177
	Appendix I. Fr John Mush's *True Report* and its History	191
	II. Sources	194
	III. Some Notes on Dates	199
	IV. Outline Pedigree of Turner, Middleton and Pope	202

All italics used in quotations are the author's.
Spelling has been modernised throughout.

Preliminary

In the early summer of 1586, a hunted priest, Fr John Mush, wrote an account of the first woman to die for the Catholic Faith in England during the reign of Queen Elizabeth I. He had been her spiritual director for the last two years of her life, after her release from her third lengthy term of imprisonment in York Castle. His work, *A True Report of the Life and Martyrdom of Mrs Margaret Clitherow*, intended both as an inspiration to contemporaries and as a record for posterity (with a view, even at that early date, to the strong possibility of her canonization as a martyr) omits much of the detail that would be included by a modern biographer.

Fr Mush saw no need to elaborate upon his subject's birth and personal circumstances. She was 'wife to Mr John Clitherow, citizen of York,' he tells us. 'She was born in York, the daughter of Mr Middleton, a man of good wealth, who had been sheriff in the same city. . . . She was about thirty years of age, . . . a plentiful mother in children, and her husband a man of competent wealth and ability.' Later he states that her mother had been 'a rich widow.' After the martyr's condemnation, he tells us, she was visited in prison by several members of the Queen's Council in the North; 'her kinsfolk and friends' also 'laboured much' to persuade her to apostatize, or at least to make a statement that would have resulted in several months' stay of execution, but she refused.

Fr Mush's earliest readers would have been well aware of the identity of these kinsfolk and friends, and would have felt no great surprise at the personal interest in her case displayed by members of the Council. Mrs Clitherow's relations and their situation and interests were as well known in York as her twelve years' defiance of them and her frequent court appearances and imprisonments. Not only had Fr Mush no need to identify these people, he was exercising a very necessary caution in suppressing their names. To name them might have increased his own dangers and difficulties, had he been caught; on the other hand, the time might have come, if the Catholic heiress had ascended the throne, when some of St Margaret's 'worldly friends' would have been anxious to change their religion.

Twice Fr Mush refers to 'this dark time', or 'the iniquity of the time' as obliging him to make general statements, to protect those whose lives were dominated by the penal laws. Certain people, while he wrote, were still living in fear that the contribution they themselves had made towards the harbouring of a priest, the charge upon which Margaret was indicted, would come to light. Margaret had refused to stand trial, and suffered the hideous penalty reserved for such a case. She gave as her reasons her desire, firstly, to prevent her children and servants from giving evidence against her, and then, to prevent the jury from finding her guilty to please the Council, and so becoming accessories to her death. A third, unspoken, reason, lay in the involvement of some of her husband's kinsfolk.

With the passage of several centuries, the exact circumstances of the life and death of Mrs Margaret Clitherow naturally fell into oblivion, from which the labours of historians, and principally, those of Fr John Morris, S.J., in the eighteen-seventies, began to recover them. The task is by no means complete; the ramifications of the saint's earthly family spread throughout the official, professional and merchant classes, whose activities are abundantly recorded in the York archives. But enough has now been recovered to define St Margaret's situation much more accurately.

With fuller knowledge of some of the individual persons concerned, including the kind of people from whom the jury panel would have been compiled, St Margaret Clitherow's point of view, and the extreme sensitivity of her conscience (which Fr Mush stresses), can be better appreciated. Moreover, acquaintance with the identity of some of her kin and their circumstances throws into stark relief her immense strength of character, her spiritual isolation, and her increasing detachment from all save God alone.

I

Family Background

A TRAVELLER approaching the city of York from the north-east in the early sixteenth century passed through open country until he reached Clifton, where scattered houses with long gardens began. Continuing along Bootham, towards the Bar, he saw, to his right, the first indication of the built-up area of the suburbs in the small houses clustering along St Marygate and facing the massive walls and corner tower of the greatest religious house in the North of England, the Benedictine Abbey of St Mary. On the left-hand side of Bootham, a short distance from the street named Gillygate, and still outside the city walls, he would see a substantial hostelry bearing the sign of 'The Angel'.

On 23 May 1531, the proprietor of this inn, one Richard Turner, made his will.[1] Committing his soul to God Almighty and to his blessed mother Our Lady St Mary, and to the holy company in heaven, he requested burial in his parish church of St Olave, before St Anne's altar, to which he bequeathed 20d. for a light. To each of the four Orders of Friars in the city of York he left 12d.

His elder son Thomas having already received the portion due to him was only left one of his gowns and a doublet; his younger son Robert, a priest, was merely bidden to defend his mother should any lawsuit arise about the will. The testator named two sons-in-law who were to lay no claim to his goods, but to be content with whatever his widow, Margaret, should give them as executrix and residuary legatee. Among the witnesses to the will was a blacksmith named John Branton.

1

Two years later, on 20 August 1533, Richard Turner added a codicil to his will, naming a third daughter, Jenett, who had in the meantime married one Thomas Middleton, who was duly warned to be content with her dowry. The will was proved in November 1534.

On 20 March 1540—shortly after the surrender of St Mary's Abbey to the King's Commissioners—Margaret Turner, widow, made her own will,[2] by word of mouth. She bequeathed her soul to God, and desired burial as nigh to her husband as might be convenient. To her daughter Jane Middleton she left six silver spoons and 'a pair of beads' (a rosary) of ivory. The bulk of her estate she left to her sons, 'Sir' Robert (the priest) and Thomas, whom she appointed her executors, 'and they to order the said goods as their conscience shall lead them'. Probate of the will was granted in November 1540.

When, in March 1567, Jane Middleton, of the parish of St Martin, Coney Street (already known to us as the mother of Saint Margaret Clitherow) gave evidence,[3] with her husband, on behalf of their parish priest in a tithe case, she declared herself to be of the age of fifty-two years, and to have lived in that parish by the space of thirty-five years. This indicates her removal to St Martin's parish in 1532, a date which tallies with the marriage of Richard Turner's daughter 'Jenett' or Jane, between 1531 and 1533.

The maternal ancestry of the saint has been found. She had two Turner uncles, one a priest; the other, Thomas, inherited the 'Angel'.

On 22 November 1558, Thomas Turner, on his deathbed, executed his own will,[4] committing his soul to Almighty God and beseeching the holy Virgin Mary and all the holy company of heaven to pray for him. At his burial in St Olave's church he desired a Mass and dirge, at the discretion of his executrix, his wife Johan.

It is clear from this will that his brother Sir Robert Turner had already died, leaving considerable property; Thomas's son Richard had apparently had some trouble with the executorship. Thomas himself had borrowed from his

daughter Anne the twenty nobles that her uncle Sir Robert
had given her — they were to be repaid — and he also had 'in
custody' £20 belonging to his son William's intended bride.
His son Richard was to be recompensed for his father's use of
the goods his uncle Sir Robert had given him, by inheriting,
after his mother's death, the house called the 'Angel'; but if
he were unwilling to accept it, the house was 'to be sold by
his mother to pay him'. (He decided to wait, and meanwhile
to manage the inn; the following year he received the freedom of the city as an innholder.)

Thomas Turner had evidently begun to offer to his children, and perhaps to others, a primitive kind of banking
service allied to estate agency, in this case profiting himself
first, but making fair arrangements for his son and daughter.
He had also acquired another house, adjacent to the 'Angel',
and this he bequeathed to his son Edward and his heirs.

Thomas Middleton, his brother-in-law, was among the
witnesses and supervisors of this will; the first supervisor
named was a man of very good social and professional
standing, 'Master Doctor Farley, my neighbour'. (Richard
Farley, LL.D., who lived in St Marygate, was a noted ecclesiastical lawyer.)

Margaret Clitherow's uncle Thomas (who was buried in
St Olave's church on 24 November 1558) had prospered
very considerably. The social status of innkeepers had been
rising steadily during this century, and in 1545 John Beane
had been elected Lord Mayor, the first to come from this
trade.

In 1560 Thomas Turner's daughter Anne (or Agnes)
married at St Olave's church a certain Thomas Jackson
(thereby qualifying for the two feather beds her father had
bequeathed her). This marriage is an important link with a
second family of the name of Turner, clearly very closely
connected with that of the innkeepers.

It is quite possible that Robert Turner, the founder of this
second family, was the brother of Margaret Clitherow's
grandfather, Richard Turner. Robert Turner was made free
of the city in 1486, as a cook (or keeper of an eating-house);

Richard Turner, not until 1504, as a smith and haberdasher (a curious combination, or sequence, of trades, which he later abandoned, as did a number of members of other crafts, for that of innkeeper). A man might still be an apprentice at the age of thirty years (as was Thomas Middleton), and a long gap between admissions to freedom cannot be used as evidence against the theory that Robert and Richard were brothers. But there is no reference to either in the other's will, and no will of a previous generation has yet been found to mention either.

The earliest suggestion of a close link between these two families occurs in Thomas Turner's will, for another of his supervisors was 'Edward Turner'; this could not be his seventeen-year-old son of that name (free in 1565, as a weaver), for he had an interest in the estate. It is almost certainly the only son of Robert Turner (free in 1554, as a scrivener). Moreover, the 'Jenet Turner' to whom Robert Turner bequeathed a silver spoon (by his will dated 14 January 1535)[5] might be identical with 'Johan' or Jane Turner, Thomas's wife. (Richard Turner's daughter Jennet or Jane had changed her name to Middleton before the date of this will.)

Robert Turner's will contains no hint of the social position he actually occupied, let alone that to which his son and grandchildren were to rise. Yet he had at one time been one of the Masters of the wealthy and important civic Guilds of St Christopher and St.George.[6]

Robert Turner lived in the parish of St Helen, Stonegate, as did his son Edward, who eventually owned two adjacent 'mansions' between the old churchyards of St Helen, Stonegate, and St Wilfrid, also other houses in Stonegate, Lendal, Blake Street and Davygate.[7] In 1559, Edward Turner served the civic office of chamberlain, as an 'innholder'. (After 1519 freemen were able to change occupations more easily.) By 1562 'Edward Turner, gentleman' was considered of sufficient means to support the office of sheriff. When, however, his name was put forward by the Common Council of the city as a candidate, 'Master Eynns, Secretary to the Queen's

4

Majesty's Council in these North Parts' came in all haste and declared to the electors that Turner was a clerk so meet and necessary for despatch of matters before the Queen's Council that his daily attendance was essential; in the name of the Lord President, therefore, he required Turner's discharge.

Two of this Edward Turner's nine children almost certainly entered a university, and in later life he was engaged in financial transactions with Secretary Eynns himself. In his will,[8] made shortly before his death in 1580, he mentioned two 'cousins'; even allowing for the vagueness of the Elizabethan use of this term, it seems that something more than a distant kinship, let alone a mere friendship, is meant. For one of these 'cousins' was Thomas Jackson (with whom the same Edward Turner is linked in another context), who had married Anne Turner, daughter of Thomas Turner (and cousin-german of Margaret Clitherow) in 1560; the other was the second husband of Jane Middleton, née Turner, Margaret Clitherow's mother.

Another point of interest is that although Robert Turner was admitted freeman in 1486 as a cook, and was still a cook in 1516 when he served as chamberlain, by the time he made his will in 1535 he was a waxchandler. This was the trade of Thomas Middleton also. The likelihood is that Middleton had been Robert Turner's apprentice and had married his niece.

What is absolutely certain is that, whereas Richard Turner's family produced a saint, Robert Turner's branch of the family, a few generations later, produced a genius, one of the glories of English literature, a man who, like Margaret Clitherow, had 'a sharp and ready wit', and was also a Catholic. A grandson of Edward Turner married Thomasine Newton, granddaughter of Miles Newton, town clerk of York (who died in 1550); one of their sixteen children, Edith Turner (1643–1733), in 1688 became the mother of ALEXANDER POPE.[9]

The ancestry of Thomas Middleton, Saint Margaret's father, has not yet been established, though more than one family of Yorkshire gentry have laid claim to him. His will,[10] dated 14 December 1560, contains bequests to each of his sons of premises in Ripon, which suggests an origin in that district. There were other Middletons in York with Ripon connections, but so far a relationship has not been found.[11] Thomas Middleton was born at the turn of the century, and began his apprenticeship at the late age of twenty-three years, becoming a freeman in 1530 and marrying Jane Turner in 1532.

His will mentions four children of this marriage: Alice, already married to Thomas Hutchinson, a locksmith (who had gained his freedom, as a spurrier, as far back as 1541, and who lived in the same parish as the Middletons, St Martin's, Coney Street), Thomas (soon to learn the trade of a tile- and brick-maker), George (still at school, later to become a draper), and Margaret (born about the year 1553, for we learn from the *Abstract* of Fr Mush's work, published in 1619, that she was 'about some eighteen years old when she married' in 1571).

Alice Hutchinson was already the mother of two children, William (born in 1557) and Agnes (born in 1559); little Agnes was to die in 1565. A child named Margaret Hutchinson was baptized at St Martin's in July 1561; perhaps she was named after her young aunt. This family appears to have removed to another parish after 1565; they drop out of the story of Margaret Clitherow.

Fr Mush stresses the wealth of Margaret's parents, which is reflected in the career of her mother's second husband, whom, according to the same authority, she 'took from the beggar's staff'; his success sprang from her wealth. Thomas Middleton kept a large staff of servants, to three of whom he bequeathed a ewe each, while to all the rest he left 12d.; in return, he asked them all to pray for him. He also left 'to the four wards of poor folks within this city, to every ward 3s.4d.' for the same purpose. By the year 1560, that was all he dared to ask.

II

Childhood

WHEN St Margaret's uncle Thomas Turner made his will in November 1558, the Catholic Queen Mary lay still unburied, awaiting elaborate obsequies in Henry VII's Chapel at Westminster. Meanwhile, the accession of her half-sister Elizabeth was being received with rejoicing by Protestants and with some apprehension by the more conservative of her subjects.

The difference of tone between Thomas Turner's will and that of his brother-in-law Thomas Middleton, made only two years later, reflects the latest disturbance in the religious situation of the English people, a further 'alteration in religion'. As the old order changed once more, confidence was replaced with uncertainty, even with fear. Thomas Turner, in beseeching the Blessed Virgin Mary and all the holy company of heaven to pray for him, was echoing the centuries-old liturgical prayers for the dying; while Masses for the dead had been used as early as the fifth century. Thomas Middleton's requests for prayer derive from a continuing belief in Purgatory, where the soul's purification and release might be hastened by the renewal of the sacrifice of Calvary in the Mass and by the intercession of the saints. All this had once more been swept away; a truly Protestant will contains no request for prayers. The 'holy and wholesome thought' of Judas Maccabeus, prayer for the dead, 'that they may be loosed from their sins' (2 Macc. 12. 46) has been condemned, and its Jewish source rejected from the Protestant Bible. Sterner and less comforting texts have come into

7

fashion: 'The dead know not any thing' (Eccles. 9. 5); 'In the place where the tree falleth, there it shall be' (Eccles. 11. 3).

The English people had been ill prepared to resist the revolutionary ideas from the Continent which had already proved a useful ally for those whose main purpose in destroying ecclesiastical institutions was private gain. The great movement known as the Reformation, originating in justifiable indignation at abuses and corruption in the Church, soon gained the support of many who had fostered in themselves a latent protest against her authority in the spheres of faith and morals. This came at a time when the practice of the Faith had become to a varying extent mechanical and materialistic.

With the revival of classical learning, an entirely new attitude to life began to develop. In both its secular and its religious manifestations it was at first largely individualistic. Loss of faith in the teaching authority of the Church, and the repudiation of her discipline, resulted on the one hand in the elevation of the 'private judgement' of individuals into innumerable contradictory authorities, and on the other in a lowering of moral standards.

In 1534, King Henry VIII, in order to obtain his divorce from Queen Catherine of Aragon, had totally withdrawn his realm from the Roman obedience; Parliament set aside the papal power and declared the King to be Supreme Head, on earth, of the Church of England. Refusal to acknowledge him in this capacity was punished as high treason; the first of a long line of Catholic martyrs suffered this penalty in May 1535.

In 1536 York was the setting for some of the most startling episodes of the confused rebellion, partly religious in motivation, known as the Pilgrimage of Grace, when the Lord Mayor and Aldermen opened the city gates to Robert Aske, its leader. In 1537 Aske was hanged at York Castle, while two monks from the London Charterhouse were hanged on the York Knavesmire for denying the royal supremacy.

Between 1536 and 1540 all the religious houses of England and Wales were suppressed and their possessions seized by the Crown; their lands were rapidly re-granted, creating great opportunities for a privileged class to enrich itself. In

8

1541 King Henry paid an impressive and punitively expensive twelve-day visit to York, receiving gifts of money and an abject apology from the Lord Mayor and Aldermen for the city's share in the rebellion.

During 1547 all colleges, free chapels, chantries, hospitals, fraternities, brotherhoods and guilds were abolished and their properties granted to King Edward VI. (The colleges of the universities of Oxford and Cambridge, also of Winchester and Eton, and the chapters of the cathedrals and of St George's, Windsor, as well as the trade guilds, were exempted.) The suppression of these smaller institutions had a greater effect on the populace at large than the loss of the monasteries. It would be difficult to overestimate the effect of the sudden destruction not only of almost all the hospitals and a large number of schools — for many of the chantry priests were running grammar schools — but also of the countless 'friendly societies', the religious guilds which benefited their own members in sickness, misfortune, old age and death, and had often assisted the community at large by the establishment of almshouses, the upkeep of highways and bridges and other useful and charitable works.

Some of the properties of the hospitals and religious guilds in York were granted to the Corporation, who also received the endowments of the guilds of St Christopher and St George, attached to the church of St Martin, Coney Street. They were able, too, to preserve the Common Hall, which they had built jointly with these guilds. Though something was saved for the community by such grants of land and houses, the intimate relationship between the members of the parochial guilds was lost and the spiritual and social life of the parish correspondingly weakened.

It had been evident from the beginning of the reign of the young King Edward VI that the Protestant Protector who had seized power would do his utmost to complete the destruction of the Catholic Church in England, not merely materially, but spiritually, by the abolition of the Mass, which was the object of the Reformers' peculiar hatred, and of almost the whole sacramental system.

Although, in the conservative North, Protestantism made comparatively little headway during Edward's reign, there were some who left the country, unable to endure the liturgical changes, the new English *Book of Common Prayer*, the preaching against their cherished beliefs and practices, and the destruction not only of the statues, but even of the altars, as symbols of the Christian sacrifice. (The high altar of York Minster, fifteen feet long, of the same blue-grey limestone as the shrine of St William—which had been destroyed in 1541—was merely transferred, upside-down, to the centre aisle of the recently-rebuilt church of St Michael le Belfrey, across the road.)[1]

In July 1553 King Edward died, and under his sister Mary the entire process of changing the religion of the English people was reversed. Soon the Mass was restored and Mary was freed from the obnoxious title of Supreme Head of the Church. In 1554, under the auspices of Cardinal Pole as papal legate, the two Houses of Parliament, expressing detestation of their 'most horrible defection and schism from the Apostolic See', acknowledged once more its supremacy.

The Faith thus restored was for the most part no more than a fitful regalvanizing of a moribund body of belief and practice. An immense task lay before Queen Mary, the true restoration and stabilization of the Catholic faith in England. The brief duration of her reign, the unpopularity of her marriage to Philip of Spain, her failure to produce an heir, and the obstinacy and cruelty with which the sick woman pursued her revenge upon Protestants, ensured that her task would not be completed. She owed her measure of success largely to the conservatism of the majority of her people.

A whole generation had by now grown up with decreasing opportunities for education. Among ordinary lay people there was a great need for instruction and even more for some kind of inspiration. The infusion of a new spirit was required; but whence should it come? Foreign visitors professed to be shocked by the attitude of the English. There was an element of truth in the report of an

Italian visiting the country towards the end of Mary's reign:
    Religion, although apparently thriving in this country, is
    I apprehend in some degree the offspring of dissimulation.
    Generally speaking, you may rest assured, that with the
    English the example and authority of the sovereign is
    everything, and religion is only so far valued as it incul-
    cates the duty due from the subject to the prince.

Queen Elizabeth I at her accession in November 1558 was
determined to 'settle' religion. That she was to some extent
committed to the reforming party was the result of the
weakness of her claim to the throne. The Act of Parliament
which declared her illegitimate was never annulled, and she
needed the support of the vociferous Protestants who flocked
back from exile at the news of Mary's death.

Yet she consistently refused to fulfil their hope of the
establishment of a Church on the Continental pattern, with,
eventually, the abolition of the episcopal office. From the
settlement of 1559, which the Protestants regarded as only
the prelude to reform, Elizabeth refused to move.

Her first Parliament restored to the Crown the temporal
headship (under God) of the Church of England. By the Act
of Supremacy, any person maintaining the spiritual or temporal jurisdiction of any foreign prince or prelate should, for
the first offence, forfeit all his property real and personal — if
he did not possess goods worth £20, he was to suffer
imprisonment for one year — for the second offence, he was
to incur the penalties of *Praemunire* (outlawry, forfeiture of
lands and goods, and imprisonment at the Queen's pleasure), and for the third offence, suffer death as a traitor. An
oath declaring the Queen's supremacy was to be imposed on
all beneficed clergy, and all judges, justices, mayors and
other laymen holding office under the crown. An act of 1563
both extended the reach of this oath of supremacy and
allegiance and increased the penalties for refusal.

By the Act of Uniformity of the same Parliament, the
second *Book of Common Prayer* of King Edward VI, with slight
but significant alterations, was reintroduced; every person

11

was to attend his parish church on Sundays and holy days, under pain of forfeiting twelve pence, twice the daily wage of a labourer, for every occasion omitted. (These fines were subsequently allocated to the poor of the parish concerned, thus reducing the new poor rate.) The ecclesiastical courts were empowered to use spiritual censures against those who refused to attend church; in practice, the High Commission punished recalcitrants by imprisonment.

The great majority of the clergy took the oath of supremacy, and for the first ten years of Elizabeth's reign there was little open resistance to the re-established religion of the English liturgy and Bible, although, in the North, many signs of the 'old religion' remained, and there was no great enthusiasm for the new ways of thought.

Elizabeth had sacrificed her personal taste, which was conservative, to prevent a war of religion in England. To strike a balance between her subjects' beliefs, to provide in the service book for two distinct doctrines in the words with which the Communion was administered, to offer a 'middle road' in religion, was to Elizabeth a matter of expediency, not of principle.

The compromise she had produced was, however, increasingly unsatisfactory to two minorities, the larger consisting of the convinced Protestant beginning to be called 'Puritan', 'the preciser sort', and the smaller, the convinced Catholic, now better instructed, who, after the ruling by Pope Pius IV forbidding attendance at the Prayer Book service, began to withdraw from church attendance and to be known as 'recusant'.

Nine months before the death of Queen Mary, Thomas Middleton, Margaret Clitherow's father, completed a three-year term of office as one of the four churchwardens of St Martin's, Coney Street.[2] As a waxchandler, he had a vested interest in the continuance of Catholic services and customs, which required the burning of candles, tapers and votive lights, so he was unlikely to become an enthusiast for the reformed religion. On the contrary, between 1555 and 1558 he was responsible for continuing the restoration of the church for the liturgy and usages of the 'old religion'.

This process had begun in the first year of Queen Mary's reign, when the churchwardens' accounts record a payment of three shillings to three tilers and their servants for setting up the high altar, of the very large sum of forty shillings to a glazier for repairing the glass windows, and of other amounts for the purchase of a chalice and paten and a holy water vat, and for painting the rood and the two statues of the Blessed Virgin and Saint John.

On Candlemas Day 1555 Thomas Middleton and his three companions took office and were soon supervising the setting up of the rood, buying candlesticks for the rood-light and having them painted, repairing the Easter Sepulchre, having six yards of haircloth made up into an altar-covering, buying charcoal for the Easter Vigil service on Holy Saturday, repairing the 'stalls' for choir and congregation, supplying an antiphoner towards the singing of the psalms, and even finding one penny 'for mending the Pax', the little prayer-board handed round at the Kiss of Peace.

These might seem no more than the actions of a conservative but materially-minded man, more intent on the profits of trade than interested in religious controversies. But there is evidence that Thomas Middleton had a respect for the office of priesthood that transcended self-interest.

His relations with Robert Fox, curate of St. Martin's from 1552 to 1557, had been sorely tried. Fox was ill-equipped for the Latin liturgy and had become an alcoholic. He was eventually brought before the ecclesiastical court, and in 1556 the parish clerk gave evidence that when he 'was helping to christen a child of one Mr Middleton's about a two years since, for where he [Fox] should have said, "*Ego baptizo te, in nomine patris* etc.", he said nothing but "*Ego baptizo te*". . .'.[3]

This case, 'begun by consent of the most part of the parishioners', was formally initiated by three of the churchwardens. Thomas Middleton, however, the fourth churchwarden, played no part in bringing the case against his errant curate, in spite of his personal involvement.

The surviving papers of another case in one of the church courts reveal the Middletons on friendly social terms with their vicar, Thomas Grayson (named as first witness to Middleton's will. Grayson, formerly a Canon Regular of Newburgh Priory and then a chantry priest at York Minster, had been described by the Chantry Commissioners in 1548 as 'meanly learned', but 'of honest conversation and qualities'.)

In 1567 Grayson confided in his wealthy parishioners his inability to obtain the small tithes, oblations and other emoluments due to him from a newcomer to the parish, and both Thomas and Jane Middleton gave independent evidence on his behalf. From these papers we learn that besides his house in Davygate and the other properties referred to in his will, Thomas Middleton also possessed a farmhold outside St Martin's parish, where his wife had once kept chickens, from which she had paid tithe in kind. (She herself had heard it said of previous incumbents of St. Martin's that 'when the parishioners sent them little chickens . . . they would send them back again'. This at least was evidence that tithe-chickens were due, and perhaps evidence also of Jane's sense of humour.)[4]

It was particularly kind of Thomas Middleton to give evidence at this time, for he was a very old and sick man, within two months of his death. He suffered from gout. So ill had he been with the gout in September 1564, when he was elected one of the two sheriffs of the city, that he could not even be present at the election, and a deputation was sent to his house where he lay upon his bed, to hear him take the customary oath of office. Two months later he was still too ill to take another oath, on his admission among the Twenty-Four, the Privy Council of the city.

Attainment of the high civic office of sheriff was a compliment to his wealth and ability, but it had great disadvantages. It entailed, among other things, being responsible for prisoners, empanelling juries for the city Quarter Sessions and Assizes, and making preparations for, and attending, all the executions of criminals condemned in the city; and it was an expensive office, never popular.

Thomas Middleton's trade was in any case much decayed as a result of the Elizabethan settlement of religion. He must have been a deeply disappointed man. When he had handed over office as churchwarden of St Martin's at Candlemas 1558, he would have felt a certain satisfaction at the refurbishment of the church, but his successors were obliged to carry out a complete reversal of policy. Early in 1561, the high altar and two side altars were taken down once more, a board bearing the Ten Commandments was erected, and 4d. was paid for the 'carrying of the images to be burned'.

This, then, was the background to Margaret Clitherow's childhood. Fr Mush, who underestimated her age, thought she had grown up in complete ignorance of the Catholic faith and Church, and the writer who abridged his work and used some other source that gave her age, refers to 'her breeding giving her knowledge of no other religion than of that [which] was publicly taught within the kingdom'. But a child of sharp intelligence, born in the year of Queen Mary's accession, might have just remembered the Mass in St Martin's church, or at least the sudden changes in the building's interior — she was eight years old when the altars and statues were removed for the second time — and, especially, her father's resentment at the third alteration of ecclesiastical policy within twelve years. She would not, of course, have understood these grown-up matters, but there must have been many strange occurrences for which she could find no explanation until, as an adult, she learned something of recent history.

One inescapable sign of changed belief was the suppression of the traditional religious pageants which had been played by members of the various trade guilds of York for two centuries. It was not with a sense of religious dedication that they acted; this was their entertainment as well as their instruction. The Creed Play and the Paternoster Play were still sometimes performed, but the great favourite was the Corpus Christi Play.

The theologians of King Edward VI had been determined to destroy belief in the Real Presence of Christ in the Sacrament of the Altar, but the tradesmen of York continued during his reign to use the term 'Corpus Christi' in the dating of their records, for it was their custom. And regardless of ecclesiastical opinion, they continued to act their beloved 'Corpus Christi Play' on the appropriate feast day, whether the feast itself was one of the 'holy days abrogated' or not.

Protestant Archbishops hardly knew how to tackle the problem of the plays: year by year, with scarcely a break, save when the sickness was rife, or when the great bridge broke and the wagons were left stranded on the far side, on the Thursday after Trinity Sunday, the whole population of York, with the exception of a handful of Protestant objectors, encamped in the streets along the route of the forty-five wagons on which the mystery plays were acted. The clergy could with difficulty interfere, for the plays had long ago passed from the control of the Church; each was performed by a different 'mystery' or trade guild, or group of guilds, under the supervision of the Corporation.

The first half of the cycle of plays covered Salvation history from the creation of the world, the fall of Adam and Eve, and three Old Testament 'types' of redemption (Noah's Ark, the sacrifice of Abraham, and the deliverance of the Jewish people from Egypt), down to Christ's entry into Jerusalem; the second half dealt with the Passion, death and victory of Christ.

All through the plays a contrast is made between loving obedience and proud disobedience. To love and worship God is shown to be man's purpose on earth, and love and obedience are almost synonymous. Supreme obedience to the will of God is rendered by the human will of God the Son Incarnate:

'If it possible were, This pain might I overpass.
But, Father, if thou see it may not,
Be it worthily wrought,
Even at thine own will . . .'

The date of the last performance of these plays is uncertain; possibly they continued to be acted, after some re-writing, until 1571. But ten years earlier, when Margaret Middleton was eight years old, they were certainly acted in full, save for the unscriptural plays of the death, assumption and corona-tion of the Virgin.

The play traditionally acted by Thomas Middleton's trade guild, the Chandlers, was the 'Shepherds' Play': 'Shepherds talking to one another, the star in the east, an angel announcing to the shepherds joy for the birth of the Child.' Much ingenuity must have gone into providing the 'star in the east', which the waxchandlers were best qualified to produce, 'a wondrous sight'.

Margaret must surely have remembered this. Her family probably had a place reserved for them to see the plays at the 'station' in the open space in front of the Common Hall. The first wagon, bearing the Tanners' play of the creation of the heavens and the angels and the fall of Lucifer, would reach this station at about half-past seven in the morning, and the others would follow at brief intervals all day, until the Mer-cers' play of the Last Judgement, with its terrifying devils in coats decked with hair and feathers, its good souls dressed in white leather coats and its bad souls in black and yellow or red and yellow garments, took place by torchlight in the evening.

But by then young Margaret Middleton must have long been fast asleep.

Not until the Queen's Council in the North could control the city Corporation would the Plays cease to be acted. This body, which originated in the fifteenth century as the private council of Richard Duke of Gloucester, who administered the North for his brother, Edward IV, had been thoroughly reorganised after the suppression of the Pilgrimage of Grace. Its purpose then was in part to answer the rebels' complaints about the law's delays and the difficulty of obtaining justice so far from the courts at Westminster; it was also intended to pacify and tame the wild and rebellious North. At first it met

17

four times a year in various large towns or cities, but by 1561 it had become stabilized at York, with headquarters at the Manor, the former palace of the abbots of St Mary's. This increased the Council's efficiency, and it gradually became not only the overriding administration, supervising the local authorities in carrying out the orders of the central government, but also the supreme court of justice North of the Trent, with a very wide civil and criminal jurisdiction. In both capacities it met with opposition, from the courts at Westminster and from resentful city councillors. However, during the Presidency of the third Earl of Huntingdon, the personnel of the city Corporation was to become more docile, much more Protestant, and more ready to obey the orders of the Privy Council in London, received through the Queen's local representative.

This long-drawn-out process of bringing the North to heel was to be the significant background to the life of Margaret Middleton.

III

Adolescence — I

THOMAS MIDDLETON died in May 1567; on the 16th of that month he was buried in St Martin's church, in the middle aisle, before the high choir; for his grave a fee of 3s.4d was paid to the churchwardens. He left to his widow a life interest in almost all his lands and leases (which after her death would revert to their children, as specified individually in his will).[1]

Mistress Middleton, sole executrix, had two men of affairs to advise her in the probate, Edward Turner and Thomas Jackson, whom her husband had appointed as supervisors. (Probate was granted on 10 June.) She was now fifty-two or fifty-three years of age, a rich widow, an excellent prize in the Tudor marriage-market for a man who was in no hurry to found a family.

Four months after her first husband's death, Jane Middleton laid aside her weeds and married a man who was her junior by perhaps thirty years. At about the same time,[2] the bridegroom, Henry May, received the freedom of the city, as an innholder.

An exceptional career lay ahead of Henry May. Fr Mush's remarks about him brand him as an adventurer, and a recent discovery tends to confirm this suggestion. For he was no Yorkshireman; he and his brother Roger (whose conduct was evidently something of an embarrassment)[3] came from Hampshire.[4] They may have arrived in the city in 1561, the year in which a new Ecclesiastical Commission for the Northern Province was established in York, which already

19

held the permanent headquarters of the Council in the North. These two factors created many new openings for innkeepers; a knowledge of the wine trade, which Henry May evidently possessed, was also essential for a man aspiring to the proprietorship of a leading inn in the city.

Southampton or Portsmouth might have provided good opportunities for advancement to a local youth, but Henry May's ambition was for higher things. By-passing London, he journeyed to the northern capital, where life was lived on a smaller but much more intimate scale. The Council in the North had almost viceregal powers, and, together with the High Commission, would increasingly make York the centre of a vast network of interests, attracting great landowners and gentry, members of all the professions, and litigants and witnesses of every class. An inn was itself a microcosm of local society. To run a great inn in York opened up vistas of power. But first a young[5] man needed money.

Henry May, a 'foreigner', gate-crashed his way into the ruling oligarchy of the city, and rose with extraordinary speed. He married on 8 September 1567; on 3 February 1568[6] he was elected one of the chamberlains, a position of trust which formed the first serious step on the ladder of civic advancement. (Most citizens did not attain to this stage, if at all, for several years after becoming freemen.) On 9 April 1568, after a dispute between the vintners and the city Corporation which led to two of their number losing their licences to retail wine, Henry May and a merchant named William Hewetson were nominated and assigned to keep taverns and also to sell wines in the city (a privilege reserved to eight persons only). Seven months after his marriage, Henry May had arrived.

He must have had something more than the power of his elderly wife's wealth (which was in fact rather precarious, depending so much on a mere life interest). He came swaggering into York with his southern speech and southern manners, a highly intelligent young man, with a readiness to serve, to act and to take responsibility that contrasted with the slower, often more reluctant, and more roundabout ways of many of his elders. He had an immense and infectious self-confidence, and probably, very considerable charm.

He certainly knew how to bide his time, to wait with patience for the flood-tide in the affairs of those around him that would lead him on to fortune. He must have been keeping his eye on the sick and aged waxchandler in Davygate, whose wife, fifteen years younger, was yet past the age of child-bearing. There would be time enough to marry again and found a family when she died; meanwhile, he would not have to budget for children. He was a calculating young man.

He swept Mrs Middleton off her feet; his very audacity must have recommended him in some quarters. His proposal had, however, a very real advantage for her, besides the acquisition of a clever young man to deal with her business affairs free of charge. Henry was anxious to turn the large Davygate house into an inn, and Jane could foresee a revival of the lively, bustling atmosphere in which she had been brought up at the 'Angel'.

Jane Middleton was still young enough to enjoy the position of hostess of an inn. (Was not her younger daughter, Margaret, later to be praised as excelling 'in every point wherein the commendation of a good housewife standeth'?) Her existing household increased with cooks, waiters, chambermaids and ostlers, she would help to control a successful business, a very different prospect from the tedium of widowhood.

By the time of his death in 1596, Henry May had built up an estate consisting of a 'house and houses now united in Coney Street extending unto Davygate' in the parishes of St Martin and St Helen, comprising 'forefronts, backfronts [sic], halls, parlours, chambers, galleries, cellars, solars, kiln, stables, backhouses, courts, yards, gardens . . . ', and containing 'wainscots, ceilings, glass, cisterns, tables, benches, forms, stools, beds with their furnitures and bedsteads, chairs, cupboards, plate, . . . utensils, brass, vessels, pewter, linen, napery and . . . other goods of household and furniture. . . .'[7] When his house had been broken and entered in 1585 it was described as a 'mansion'.[8]

On the death of his wife Jane in that year and the reversion of her property to her children, he evidently recovered lost ground by a swift remarriage with Anne Thomson,[9] who was already his servant.[10] (Soon afterwards she, and not her husband, was responsible for the burial of Maud, daughter of the celebrated woodcarver, alderman and one time Lord Mayor of York, Thomas Drawswerde, in her father's tomb in St Martin's churchyard;[11] this suggests very strongly that Anne was the great-granddaughter of Thomas, and the great-niece of Maud Drawswerde, and presumably heiress to some of the family properties in Davygate.[12])

Fr Mush, who, in spite of his tendency to vituperate Protestants, knew well the limits imposed by the classification of calumny and detraction as mortal sins, says that Henry May's previous adultery with Anne Thomson was notorious;[13] and he was writing in the first place for those familiar with the local situation. It seems that Henry had seduced Anne to make sure of winning her as his second wife, for reasons of policy. The notoriety of the offence would simply strengthen his hand.

When he made his will in June 1596, Henry May referred to 'those lands and goods whereof and wherewith it hath pleased the Almighty to endue me'; but there is no doubt that he had himself made a vigorous contribution towards their acquisition.

With the entrance of such a man as this into the Middleton family in 1567, the whole atmosphere of Margaret's home changed; within four months, an ailing, probably cantankerous, gout-afflicted, aged man was replaced by a young, healthy and lively man, full of new ideas and plans, who wasted no time in carrying them out. He had gained a family of four children, two of whom were young enough to be both influenced and used. (George in particular was of an age to make a hero of him.) His stepdaughter was now aged about fourteen years; she cannot have failed to appreciate her stepfather's intelligence and capacity. Perhaps the high-spirited and headstrong girl enjoyed a friendly battle of wits from time to time with him, for she had probably been rather spoiled as the youngest child of elderly parents. Henry May would certainly wish to placate her in what could have been a very tense and difficult domestic situation. (She did in fact hold the key to his fortune, for under the terms of her father's will, the all-important, city-centre house in Davygate was to become her property on the death of her mother.)

Margaret was growing into a lovely young woman: 'to her beautiful and gracious soul God gave her a body with comely face and beauty correspondent'. And as she grew older, it is likely that she was obliged to rebuff Henry May's attempts at undue familiarity with her. 'Let him remember,' says Margaret's biographer rather ominously, in connection with Henry May's final slanders on her character, 'whether he himself had not good proofs of' her 'constant honesty at all times when she was in her mother's house.'

Margaret, after her conversion, daily looked back in penitence upon 'her youth spent out of the Catholic Church of Christ, in vain follies and schism', convinced that for years she had dishonoured God. She had learned 'to serve only the world vainly'. Her own father's wary resentment at the liturgical changes can have given her no very clear ideas on religion, but her stepfather's opinions must have influenced her considerably during her adolescence. For Henry May was, or claimed to be, a Protestant. Without trying to open a window into that dark soul, we may point out that every step he was to take to implement the government's persecution of Catholics led to his own advancement; it will later be seen how eagerly he became the tool of the Lord President of the Council in the North (himself a convinced Protestant) and how unscrupulously he increased the subservience of the city of York to the Council *in defiance of his instructions*.

His will reveals none of the uncertainty long felt in the conservative North by the reluctant conformist; he prays to be made 'one of that number that shall reign in [Christ's] kingdom prepared in his mercy for his own elect', a Calvinistic phrase. It is noticeable, however, that he does not mention a single book, none of those volumes of godly theology or of virtuous exhortation beloved by the true Protestant, not so much, even, as a Bible. But he was undoubtedly a Protestant inasmuch as, being guided so largely by self-interest, he naturally favoured the winning side.

IV

Adolescence — II

EARLY in 1568, soon after Henry May had entered
upon office as one of the eight chamberlains of York,
the Corporation decided that the pageant to be performed this year, should be the Creed Play, which had
evidently not been acted for a long time. It was to be
provided for and brought forth by the oversight and order of
the chamberlains, who were instructed to obtain the master
copy of the play, to find the best players and to have the parts
written out for each to con. They were 'further to see all
manner the pageants, playing gear and necessaries to be
provided in a readiness, and as occasion shall require to ask,
advise and aid about the same'. They were also to collect the
accustomed pageant-money from each of the crafts usually
concerned with the production of the Corpus Christi Play.

However, when Dean Hutton, consulted rather late, read
the text of the play, which was entirely new to him, he was
taken aback. He told the Lord Mayor and his Brethren, 'as I
find many things that I much like because of the antiquity, so
I see many things that I cannot allow, because they be
disagreeing from the sincerity of the Gospel. . . .' He therefore urged 'that it should not be played; for though it was
plausible forty years ago, and would now also of the ignorant
sort be well liked, yet now in this happy time of the Gospel, I
know the learned will mislike it, and how the State will bear
with it I know not. . . .' The text of the Creed Play was never
seen again.

The Corporation, doubtless feeling very flat, decided to

have no play at all this year. But in April the Common
Council petitioned the Lord Mayor and Aldermen to have
the Corpus Christi Play performed. A compromise was
agreed upon: that the Dean should be asked to amend the
(already mutilated) Corpus Christi Play. He agreed, and the
amended version was performed in 1568 and 1569.

To Henry May, reluctantly involved at least in collecting
the pageant-money, the mystery plays must have been a
matter of amazement and contempt from the time he first
came to York. The south of England could show nothing to
compare with this. His household must have been informed
of his opinions of the plays, both as rags of popery and as a
wicked, ridiculous and time-wasting extravagance. However, they did bring visitors into the city, and the inns were
packed.

As it happened, the two guilds relevant to his own occupation, the Vintners and the Ostlers or Innholders, had each at
some stage been deprived of its play; the Vintners', dealing
with the Marriage Feast of Cana, has been entirely lost,
clearly because the traditional parallel with the Eucharistic
theology underlying the plays was too obvious. The Ostlers'
play of the Assumption of the Blessed Virgin into Heaven
has survived, but was removed from the acting programme
in 1561. So Henry May probably was never called upon to
pay pageant-money himself.

With his marriage to Jane Middleton, Henry May
acquired useful kinsfolk. Connections by marriage amongst
the governing class of the city were as much a social cement
as blood relationships. So, immediately, he was linked to two
men who were rising rapidly, not in the ranks of the city's
government, but in the offices and courts of the Council in
the North. These were Edward Turner (who, we have seen,
was possibly as close as cousin-german to Jane Middleton)
and Thomas Jackson, who had married Jane's niece Anne
Turner in 1560. Edward Turner the scrivener-clerk by 1572
was responsible for examining the Council's decrees and
other documents before the Secretary counter-signed them,[1]

while the younger Jackson, an attorney, was practising in the Council's courts. Before many years had passed, Turner was deeply involved in property speculation, not only with Secretary Eynns, but with Henry May.

The Council in the North was soon to reach its apogee of power, influence and success under the Presidency of the third Earl of Huntingdon. During this period (1572–95) its staff appear to have numbered some hundred persons, and its dependents (their families) a further two hundred. They not only helped to restore prosperity to the city, which had been through a long period of economic depression, but improved the social life of the citizens, who had a passion for banquets and every sort of entertainment.

At one time, the Corporation had resolved to economize on feasting, but not to abolish it altogether, 'because meeting of neighbours at the said feasts and dinners and there making merry together was a good occasion of continuing and renewing of amity and neighbourly love one with another'. By 1584 York was a-hum with amusements, fit to compare, for merry pastime and company, with any other city in the realm, save only London; so sang a certain William Elderton, in a well-known broadsheet celebrating in particular a week-long archery contest between rival teams of the Earls of Essex and Cumberland.

> I passe not[2] for my monie it cost,
> Though some I spent and some I lost,
> I wanted neither sod nor roast,
>   As if it had been in London.
> For there was plentie of every thing,
>   Redd and fallowe deere, for a king,
> I never saw so mery shooting,
>   Since first I came from London.[3]

Betting was already the accompaniment of many a sport such as this. As early as 1568 the Corporation had appreciated the benefit of agreeing to the request of divers worshipful gentlemen to have a cockpit made in York 'that they might resort unto for their pastime and to spend their money here that they were wont to spend in other places'; it was made in the former garden of the Augustinian Friars.

Margaret Clitherow had, according to Fr Mush, 'many worldly friends'. It is easier to identify her cousins, of whatever degree, and whether 'worldly' or otherwise, the children of her uncle Thomas Turner and of her 'cousin' Edward Turner. Her cousin-german Richard, proprietor of the 'Angel' in Bootham, survived until 1579, leaving a daughter Anne, who died unmarried in 1588. Her cousin Anne, married to Thomas Jackson, had a large number of children, several of whom died, and died herself in 1577. Her cousin Alice, born in 1549, married Miles Tompson in 1576. Her cousin Edward (not to be confused with the examining-clerk) obtained the freedom of the city as a weaver in 1565, but by 1571, when he was forced, much against his will, to become one of the sheriffs, he was an innkeeper (possibly running the 'Angel' for his eldest brother). A sickly man, he was dead by 1580. The fate of his brothers William and John is not known. Margaret's aunt Agnes, married to Richard Wood, was living in Marygate at her death in 1588. Her other aunt, of unknown name, the widow of John Joye (who had died in 1558) had at least one child, Robert, born in 1551. The widow of Margaret's uncle Thomas, Johan or Jane Turner, continued to live at the 'Angel' until her death in 1575.

Margaret's more distant 'cousin' Edward Turner, who lived close to Davygate, had eight surviving children. The eldest son, Lancelot, matriculated in 1564 at Trinity College, Cambridge, where his youngest brother, Martin, also matriculated twenty years later. Edward Turner's son Thomas was made free of the city in 1580 as a goldsmith, his son Philip in 1586 as a merchant. His son Edward was still a child in 1580, when his father made his will, shortly before his death. Edward Turner senior had three daughters: Margaret married a man named Willowbie, and on his death married John Stephenson (already a supervisor of her father's will) in 1581; she had several children (Joan, Anne, Elizabeth and Thomas Willowbie, and William and John Stephenson); Elizabeth Turner married, firstly, in 1580, Lancelot Martin, by whom she had two children, Thomas and Margaret, and secondly a man named Hustler, by whom she had a son, John; Edward's youngest daughter, Katherine, married Thomas Blenkarne, another clerk to the Council in the North, in 1582.

Edward Turner senior had one sister, Alice, who married John Hall (evidently her father's former apprentice, a wax-chandler) and was widowed in 1577.

Edward Turner's first wife, the mother of his children, died in 1571, and the following year he married Jane Fale, widow of the former town clerk, Thomas Fale, who had also died in 1571. This lady, who survived until 1589, left a lengthy will which gives some indication of the wealth of the circle in which Margaret Clitherow's 'worldly friends' moved.

The very large sum of £30 was to be bestowed upon her funeral. She left a total of £8.6s. to prisoners and the poor and towards the repair of highways. Distributed in a great many legacies, she left twenty 'old angels', four French crowns, one 'portigue' (a Portuguese gold coin), one old riall, and twenty marks (£13.6s.8d.), and a further total of £34.3s.4d., also 3s.4d. to every servant, and 2s. to every godchild who asked for it.

She specifies some of her jewellery: a gold ring with a sparkled diamond and a ruby in it, a silver-gilt tablet with pearls, a gold ring with a yellow stone, a gold ring with a death's head therein, a tablet of gold (which had belonged to Edward Turner, her late husband), two flat gold rings and a hoop ring.

Then her clothes! Her best gown and her best damask kirtle, her black gown furred with black coney, her better buffin gown, her black cloth gown guarded with velvet, her crane-collared kirtle of damask and her best red petticoat with silk fringe, her second red petticoat fringed with crewels and her forekirtle of grosgrain laid with silk lace and fringe, her gorgettes. . . .

It was to such a style of conspicuous wealth, reflected in the luxuries allowed to his womenfolk, that Henry May aspired, yet he could proceed no further than the edge of this social circle so long as he was building up his capital and pouring the profits of his inn into real estate. His chosen occupation furthered his career as much as his marriage did, for such an inn as his was the meeting-place of every kind of business interest; the city had always attracted a very large number of day-visitors, for whom stabling, as well as food and drink, had to be provided.

To look ahead a little, the will of Edward Turner, the examining-clerk, made on 27 November 1580, reveals with startling clarity the progress made by Henry May after thirteen years of marriage; he was evidently exercising that primitive form of banking service and estate agency that a previous generation of innkeepers, such as Thomas Turner, had begun to develop. 'To my well-beloved cousin, Mr Henry May', Edward Turner made a very considerable bequest: 'the moiety of my leasehold lands in the lordship of Kexby, for that he in truth did disburse the one half of the money for the obtaining of the leases; the other moiety I give to my children, Edward, Martin and Katherine Turner; and whereas the said Henry May hath likewise a lease of certain lands in Kexby aforesaid, for the obtaining whereof [I] the said Edward Turner paid the half of the money', his will is that the said Henry May, according to his promise now made, shall assign the moiety thereof to the said Edward, Martin and Katherine Turner. (This elaborate process, based upon private agreements and mutual trust, suggests a means of evading involvement in usury, which was rampant in York at this period.)

Henry May did inspire trust among his peers; the pioneer innkeeper who was the first to become Lord Mayor (and held the office twice), John Beane, in 1579 appointed him as one of the five supervisors of his will, who were to distribute £200 to the poor at their own discretion. Henry May, together with his stepson George Middleton (and his wife) and nine others, were to have expensive mourning gowns to wear at his funeral.

Henry May was able to support the office of sheriff as early as 1570, but for details of his financial activities we can only rely on such evidence as has survived and is either readily accessible in manuscript or else has been published. In 1578, for example, he purchased a house with lands in Hinderwell, on the north Yorkshire coast, near Staithes; this can only have been for investment. He must have been successfully involved in many such business transactions; by 1580 he was on the verge of becoming an alderman, another expensive and burdensome civic office.

V

Marriage

THE first four years of Henry May's marriage, while his stepdaughter was still at home, covered a period of great interest, tensions and excitements in the North of England. In October 1568 a great Conference was, by the Queen's appointment, held in York to decide what course of action should be taken with the Catholic heir presumptive to the throne, Mary, Queen of Scots, who, having fled from her own people, who accused her of terrible deeds, was now a prisoner in England.

Henry May could congratulate himself on his perspicacity in coming to the northern capital: the city was filled to capacity with fine gentlemen from the Court accompanied by their liveried retinues and crowds of attendants, and with Scottish nobles too. The Duke of Norfolk was there (secretly nursing his ambition to marry the Queen of Scots), so were the Earl of Sussex, recently appointed Lord President of the Council in the North, and the Earl of Northumberland (possibly staying at his dilapidated mansion in Walmgate). On the Scottish side, the Regent, Murray, the Bishop of Ross, the Earl of Morton, Lord Herries, and many others attended.

Margaret Middleton, aged fifteen years, saw these events, no doubt, through the eyes of the Protestant head of her household, who said Mary was a Papist and a murderous whore. Angry he may have been to think that any conference was necessary, but there was no denying that it was very good for business, and his inn was packed out. The Lord

Mayor had made proclamation that every innholder should 'keep one ordinary table sufficiently furnished with boiled or sodden [meat] and two kinds of roast meat, bread and ale or beer', but he was not to charge more that sixpence a meal, which was annoying. However, he did a roaring trade in wines.

During the following year rumours began to circulate at court suggesting a dangerous alliance between religious malcontents in the North and certain political malcontents in the Privy Council. There appeared to be a plot involving the Duke of Norfolk; Queen Elizabeth, seriously alarmed, had him arrested and imprisoned in the Tower. Then she summoned the Catholic Earls of Northumberland and Westmorland to court. This seemed to them the prelude to a similar fate, leading to death, yet to come to court with armed followers would be offensive. They ignored the summons, which was repeated. Thereupon the two Earls raised the standard of rebellion at Brancepeth and marched on Durham, where High Mass was sung once more in the cathedral.

In the city of York there was a sense of growing uneasiness and excitement. The Lord Mayor, at the command of the Lord President, summoned the innholders, including Henry May, to a meeting, at which they were asked whether they had overheard any news, tales, reports or rumours sounding to any sedition; they were told to give a diligent ear to the conversation in their houses and to report any such talk.

Soon it was common knowledge that the Earls had raised a rebellion and were marching southwards towards York. It looked as though the Pilgrimage of Grace was about to be repeated.

The second great northern rising for the Catholic faith owed much of its strength to the Earl of Northumberland. Thomas Percy, seventh Earl, was the last of the great Border barons on whose power the defence of England from the Scots had largely depended, a power whose very existence now challenged the authority of the central government. He and the young Earl of Westmorland planned to free Mary,

Queen of Scots, 'thereby to have some reformation in religion,' as Northumberland said, 'or at the least some sufferance for men to use their conscience as they were disposed'. According to rumour, the furtherance of the Duke of Norfolk's ambition to marry Mary was associated with the plot, though Northumberland later denied that he had either approved of the suggested marriage or planned to depose Elizabeth.

In Yorkshire those who actively supported the rebellion came almost exclusively from the tenantry, relations and clients of the Earl of Northumberland. The rebels marched through Darlington to Ripon and Wetherby, and assembled on Clifford Moor, near Tadcaster, within striking distance of Mary's prison at Tutbury.

Meanwhile in the city of York the Earl of Sussex, as Lord-Lieutenant, was issuing orders that effectively prevented any repetition of the events of 1536. The Bars of the city were hastily repaired and a strong guard put upon them night and day to man the cannon, while earth and stones were set against the posterns, placing the citizens in a state of siege. All ladders were brought in from the suburbs, whose inhabitants were ordered to take shelter in the city. Boats were removed from the river banks and the approaches guarded with great guns. Lights were to be placed in house windows. Musters were held and arms and armour checked. A great many soldiers were billeted in the city and the innkeepers were warned to have bread, ale and victual meat in readiness for them.

It was a worrying time and tension was great. Food was short despite the wardens' arrangements. Every man, woman and child pent in the crowded city was given instructions on how to behave 'whensoever any alarm shall happen': they were not to 'make any shouting, crying or noise, but to keep silence'.

Henry May conveyed this warning to his womenfolk. There was much to annoy and irritate Henry these days for he at least was not 'addicted to the rebels', and his business was suffering.

The Earls did not, however, dare to attack the city. Mary, Queen of Scots, had been removed to another prison and was now beyond their reach. Seeing no great response from Catholics in other parts of the country, and unable to provide for their own troops, they retreated, and were soon in flight before the royal forces. Northumberland and Westmorland escaped for a time across the Scottish border.

By Christmas 1569 the rebellion had been completely crushed and life could return to normal. The shared apprehensions of this experience, almost of civil war, must have drawn together the diverse members of Henry May's household, and created a sense of gratitude for his vigorous and resourceful presence.

The pattern of the Pilgrimage of Grace was repeated in the revenge that followed the rebellion, in 1570, when several hundred men, almost all 'of the meanest of the people', from the villages and towns which had supported the Earls, were hanged by martial law. Some of the leaders were tried in York by a special commission, and four were executed there.

In February 1570 Henry May was chosen to be one of the four churchwardens of St Martin's, Coney Street, once more following in the footsteps of Thomas Middleton. He served a three-year term. The churchwardens straightway completed the task of removing all possible vestiges of Catholicism. (To replace the eloquent stained glass would have been too expensive, so that has survived.)

They sold the silver-gilt chalice and paten, and bought a silver communion cup. Then they spent 8d. on 'a book against the late rebellion', presumably a printed pamphlet. In January 1571 they had the rood-loft pulled down; this was evidently a difficult and even dangerous task, and 'Mr May's brother', Roger (who never became a freeman) earned 12d. for his two days' work in this connection.

Long before September, when the new archbishop, Grindal, made his primary visitation, all the offending objects had been removed. After the visitation, the churchwardens and 'sworn men' dined at Mr May's. Soon Mr

May, now Sheriff, was supplying the church with large quantities of communion wine.

He was to serve a second two-year period as church-warden, from 1579 to 1581; after this a new pew was made for 'Mr Alderman May', his newly-acquired honour. He was also made a trustee of the parish estates, being joined in this charge later by his stepson, George Middleton.

It was during his first term as churchwarden, in 1571, that Henry May had to deal officially with John Clitherow, who was serving as one of the two bridgemasters. The church-wardens of St Martin's were obliged to make an annual payment of 10d. to the bridgemasters for two common lanes. (Unlike the majority of men chosen to be bridgemasters, John Clitherow went on to be a chamberlain in 1574.)

Whether Henry May was already acquainted with John Clitherow, perhaps as a supplier of meat to his inn, is not known. They remained on good terms until Henry May's death; he left John Clitherow the gold signet ring that he wore on his little finger. But Henry was evidently on more intimate terms with his stepson George than with his son-in-law, who was perhaps a simpler and rather more countrified person.

On 1 July 1571 Margaret Middleton married John Clitherow at St Martin's church; no doubt she was given away by her stepfather, who was both churchwarden and sheriff at the time. No doubt, also, it was a very grand wedding, the sheriff being accompanied by his two sergeants-at-mace, a ceremonial point upon which Henry May was later to insist.

He had astutely chosen for his stepdaughter a husband who would never be a rival to himself, for John Clitherow was a butcher, and butchers never became aldermen. He was, however, a man 'of competent wealth and ability' — as we should expect — and a widower with two young sons, William (born in 1563)[1] and Thomas. He had been made freeman in 1560, so was very much older than his bride.

His father, Richard Clitherow, had been a tailor; in 1533, at the age of thirty years, had been one of the Keepers or trustees of the great civic Guilds of St Christopher and St George.[2] He rose to be Master of the Company of Tailors and

37

Drapers. He appears to have been a man of strong feeling: in 1551 he appeared in the court of the Lord Mayor, charged with insulting an alderman (John Lewes, a fellow-tailor, and the previous year's Lord Mayor) by refusing to raise his cap to him. 'Openly he called him churl, and if he had called him poller [extortioner], he had said but truth; and asked this audience whether he should cap to him whom he had rather fight with than otherwise, or whom he cannot love.' For this offence against the elaborate conventions emphasizing social inequalities, Richard Clitherow was committed to ward.

On the other hand, his will,[3] executed on 11 September 1564, gives the impression that he was a very loving father. He mentions three sons (John, William — whose opinions and activities would later be of some interest to the authorities — and Edmund[4]) and six daughters: the two youngest, Millicent and Mary, he 'bequeathes', as he puts it, 'Millie' to her godmother, Mrs Weddell, and Mary 'to my sister Drew, if she will have her, or else to my son John'. (John's first wife, Matilda or Maud, née Mudd, was still alive, but she did not have to take Mary, as her aunt Drew accepted her.) He makes John his sole executor, Edmund being under age, and William, trained as a lawyer's clerk, having left York (his legacy was a bay filly).

John Clitherow made a loving and remarkably tolerant husband for Margaret; he was, however, a rather materially-minded man, a full-blooded one, who loved company and feasting and was apt to talk indiscreetly in his cups. Not that he drank more that was good for him: he lived to a very great age, for a sixteenth-century man.[5]

It was to a house in the Shambles, the traditional butchers' district, that John Clitherow took his young bride, and the identification of that house and its neighbours is important to an understanding of the situation that finally brought Margaret to an appalling death. The house belonged to the Dean and Chapter of York, its rents being appropriated to the Minister Fabric Fund, and it was situated on the eastern side of the street.[6] Many rent rolls for the street survive, and from these the tenancies can be reconstructed.

The name of John Clitherow first appears in 1568 (after a

ten-year gap in the records). At the time of his second marriage the tenants of the house adjoining his own on either side were Humfrey Wayne and John Smythe, but from 1576 both these houses were occupied by relations of John Clitherow.

John was later to be involved in an extensive series of tithe suits; the surviving papers[7] reveal that for many years he had kept flocks of one or two hundred sheep on his pasture grounds at Whitwell in the parish of Crambe, Sutton-on-the-Forest, and Cornbrough in the parish of Sheriff Hutton. The last-named estate had been inherited from his father. In 1581 it was stated that his mansion-house there lay 'betwixt the common of Sutton . . . and the water called Foss'. The aged vicar of Sutton gave evidence that John's holding lay on the north-east side of the Foss.[8] John had a staff of servants there but rarely slept there himself. A husbandman of Sutton, named Thomas Batter, under interrogation, declared that he well knew John Clitherow's dwelling-house in the Shambles and had bought 'divers things upon him there at divers times'. More often, though, he would have bought them from John's wife.

The marriage of Margaret Middleton and John Clitherow was of a rather unconventional nature, for sixteenth-century York. Henry May, coming in as a foreigner, did not hesitate to marry off his stepdaughter into the most clannish of all the trades. The butchers intermarried more than the members of any other craft, and half the residents in the Shambles were closely interrelated.

The tailor Richard Clitherow having married a daughter of John Weddell, a butcher, and having apprenticed his son to a butcher, had a butcher's wife for a sister-in-law (she married William Drew) and another butcher's daughter for a daughter-in-law (Matilda, daughter of Walter Mudd). John Clitherow's cousin, another John Weddell, a butcher, married Ann, daughter of Robert Tesimond, a butcher. (The pattern will later be seen repeated among the recusant wives of butchers.)

Life in the Shambles was therefore much stranger to Margaret Clitherow than it had been to most of the other butchers' wives. Her neighbours, and even her husband, must at first have felt a little awe at the entrance among them of a young lady of superior class, with many wealthy friends and well-placed connections. But Margaret possessed qualities of great assistance to her in adjusting to her new way of life: an unconquerable gaiety, a sense of humour that enabled her to see the funny side of things (even, later, in circumstances of the utmost gravity and danger to herself), and a whole-hearted application to whatever she undertook.

Eventually, Margaret proved, according to Fr Mush, 'inferior to none of her neighbours in any honest, comely, womanly or decent quality, and worthy to be preferred before them in every point wherein the commendation of a good housewife standeth'. Meanwhile, those neighbours would take a kindly interest in the young bride and would help her to learn her household duties and responsibilities, especially as her husband was frequently absent from home on the long journeys which the wholesale side of his business entailed, also at his estates and grazing lands closer to York.

The wife of John Clitherow was obliged to take charge of his retail business, the shop that occupied the ground floor of his house in the Shambles, and there would be much for Margaret to learn here, the current prices of joints and the different cuts of meat; though she would have learned something of this in her cookery lessons. She may also have sold pies and other by-products of a butcher's business. She would have to keep a sharp eye on the servants and apprentices too. John Clitherow came to trust her absolutely, knowing she had his interests entirely at heart. He 'committed all to her trust and discretion'.

John delighted to take his lovely young wife to 'banquets'. Sometimes these would be private parties in a neighbour's house, sometimes ceremonial dinners of the Butchers' Company, held at the Butchers' Hall. And no doubt John Clitherow would often be invited with his wife to 'feast' at the Common Hall in Coney Street, that Hall built jointly by the Corporation and the Guilds of St Christopher and St George, where the Assizes for the city were held twice a year, and where, now, interludes were beginning to be performed by itinerant companies of players.

Easy as Margaret's life could have been, had she wished — for it is clear that her husband had plenty of money and bestowed it freely upon her, and that she had an adequate staff of servants — she may sometimes have sighed at the change in her surroundings. She had moved away from an inn, itself a centre of social life, in one of the most important parishes in York, where people of fashion and high social standing, including her friends, dwelt, and she now lived in a quarter occupied for many centuries by the butchers and the members of other necessary but rather unpleasant trades. (The fishmongers were quite close, with their market between Foss Bridge and St Denys's church; the air had to be sweetened when the Lord President was obliged to take that route into the city, and Henry May was later to use frankincense for this purpose.) One of the commonest sights in the district was of sheep being led to the slaughter in the Shambles.[9]

In the Middle Ages, when an attempt was made to supernaturalize every trade involved in the mystery plays, the butchers had been allocated the play of the Death of Christ; 'and blood ran down', as a spectator reminisced.

Henry May had found a complacent, trustworthy person to marry the young woman who had reversionary rights to the property he occupied. But Margaret had some cause to resent, if that had been her nature, the manner in which her stepfather had disposed of her life: within and without the shop, in that street rarely touched by the sun, she was constantly obliged to pick her way through sawdust and blood.

VI

Conversion

WITHIN three years of her marriage, while she was still no more than twenty-one years of age, Margaret Clitherow made the most crucial decision of her life. It was, as Fr Mush tells us, with considerable understatement, 'not without contradiction of her worldly friends' that she 'carefully employed herself' to obtain instruction in the religion now proscribed in England. Her motive was 'to learn her Christian duty in truth and sincerity'.

A convert can usually look back upon some single event, some point of time at which all his previous experience is seen in a new light. Fr Mush refers vaguely to the moment when Margaret 'heard first of the Catholic faith and Church', but she must already have heard a great deal about it from her stepfather, from the Protestant point of view. She had learned an 'erroneous faith', Fr Mush says, from 'the new apostate ministers'; Henry May had probably seen to it that she accompanied him and her mother to the special sermons at the Minster. For the vicar of St Martin's, her father's old friend Thomas Grayson, was not a strong candidate for conversion to Protestant doctrine; in 1567, the eventful year that brought Henry May into the family, he was in trouble with the High Commission for having Catholic books in his possession.[1]

When, at last, after learning 'to serve only the world vainly', Margaret began, away from the influence of her stepfather, to think for herself and to look around her, she realised that the violent upheaval of which both the preaching and the dangers of the recent rebellion had made her aware had resulted from a movement of comparatively recent origin 'a war and trial in God's Church', which was still in progress. She began to give critical attention to 'the ministers of the new gospel' and found 'no substance, truth nor Christian comfort' in their doctrine. She heard also that many priests and lay people were suffering for the defence of the ancient Catholic Faith.

An incident that took place in June 1572 must have struck Margaret very forcibly, for it illustrated so well the divisions that were appearing in families and destroying old friendships. It may be remembered that when, in 1531, Margaret's grandfather, Richard Turner, had executed his will, a certain John Branton had been among the witnesses. In 1541, Branton's son Nicholas had appeared on behalf of the wife of Margaret's uncle, Thomas Turner, in a defamation case heard in the Dean and Chapter's court.[2] Generation after generation of Brantons became blacksmiths, and as Richard Turner had originally obtained his freedom as 'smith and haberdasher', he may have had some craft-connection with John Branton. The two families had apparently been quite close neighbours.

John Branton had a second son, Stephen, who was also a blacksmith. On 4 June 1572 Stephen Branton appeared before the High Commission, who, because he expressly refused to communicate or to come to the church to hear divine service, committed him to ward 'to Mr. Turner, one of the sheriffs of the city of York',[3] to be kept close prisoner in the Sheriffs' Kidcote on Ouse Bridge. So began an incarceration which was to last for nearly twenty years, ending only with Stephen's death in Hull in 1591.

The Mr Turner made responsible for his safe keeping was Margaret's first cousin, Edward, the weaver (now an innholder), who had reluctantly accepted the office of sheriff in September 1571.

However instructive and shocking the punishment of Stephen Branton may have appeared to Margaret Clitherow, the impact of the beheading of Thomas Percy, seventh Earl of Northumberland, within a hundred yards of her home, at 3 p.m. on 22 August 1572, was something she could not have escaped. She may, indeed, have been an eye-witness, for the robust Elizabethans attended executions almost as a matter of course; but perhaps she shrank from this, for she 'exceeded in compassion', or perhaps the birth of her first child, a son, prevented her. (He was given the name of Henry, which indicates that Henry May was his god-father.) But as long as she was in her house she would be horribly aware of what was in progress a hundred yards away, where the lower end of the Shambles ran into the Pavement, past the church of Holy Cross. (The Pavement was in fact the market place where Margaret shopped for butter, cheese, eggs and poultry.)

Early in the morning of this day she would hear the hammering of workmen erecting the scaffold, and soon there would be a great concourse of spectators pushing their way past her window, and later flowing back up the street. She would be conscious of the excitement in the air, the unnatural hush as the executioner raised his axe, the great thundering groan of prayer and of relieved tension as he lifted the gory head and displayed it to the people.

As one of the two leaders of the Northern Rebellion of 1569, the Earl had been purchased from the Scots, among whom he had taken refuge, for the sum of £2,000, condemned by Act of Attainder, without trial, and brought back to York to bear witness, by his death, to the fate that lay in store for those who carried too far their discontent with Queen Elizabeth's settlement of the religion of her people.

By insisting on the public execution of the Earl of Northumberland in York, the government, or the Queen, produced the very opposite effect from their intention. His capture had increased still further the sympathy felt for him in the North, where he had been 'beyond measure dear to the whole people'. Then the manner of his death, so far from terrifying the citizens into conformity, showed them a religion worth dying for. The Elizabethans were connoisseurs of death; the public execution of a criminal appealed above all to their sense of the dramatic. The death of Thomas

Percy was, for dignity and courage, unlike any death they had yet seen. 'It was thought very wonderful that, from the moment of his laying himself upon the block, he gave not even the smallest sign of fear, and made no movement whatsoever, either of head or body.'

The Earl's last address, a more public profession of the Catholic faith than had been heard in York for many years, directed his hearers to the source of his courage and his consolation, namely, 'That Church which, throughout the whole Christian world, is knit and bound together. . . . In this same faith,' he said, 'I am about to end this unhappy life. But as for this new English church, I do not acknowledge it.'

To Palmer, the minister who interrupted him here, saying, 'You are dying an obstinate Papist; a member, not of the Catholic, but of the Roman Church,' the Earl replied, 'That which you call the Roman Church is the Catholic Church, which has been founded on the teaching of the Apostles, Jesus Christ himself being its corner-stone, strengthened by the blood of Martyrs, honoured by the recognition of the holy Fathers; and it continues always the same, being the Church against which, as Christ our Saviour said, the gates of Hell shall not prevail.' He declared that 'if he had a thousand lives he would give them up for the Catholic faith.'

Before his death the Earl 'begged all present to forgive him, declaring that he on his part forgave all from his heart'. He knelt down and finished his prayers, then, 'after kissing a cross, which he traced upon the ladder of the scaffold, with his arms so folded on his breast as to form a cross, he stretched himself upon the block; and as soon as he had said, "Lord, receive my soul!" the executioner struck off his head.' The weeping spectators, with one voice 'called on God to receive his soul into eternal rest'; then they swarmed about the scaffold gathering up his blood with handkerchiefs and linen cloths, as relics of a martyr.

Thomas Percy had been offered his life if he would renounce his faith — for a spectacular apostasy was worth far more than an execution — but he preferred death. It is for this and not for sponsoring a Catholic rebellion that he has been officially recognised as a martyr; and so the opinion of those who knew and loved him has been confirmed.

The same night the body of Thomas Percy, seventh Earl of Northumberland, was buried in the church of Holy Cross, at the end of the Shambles, while his head was set up on a high pole on Micklegate Bar. But before this was done, while the head lay in the Tollbooth on Ouse Bridge, a certain William Tesimond, a saddler, of the parish of St Michael le Belfrey, approached it and cut some hair off the beard. Called before the Court of High Commission in November 1572 to account for his possession of this relic, and his refusal to come to church or to communicate, he was also asked why he had referred to Thomas Percy as the 'good' Earl of Northumberland. Avoiding the trap which would have involved him in a charge of treason, he replied 'that he so writ him *for that he made so good an end*'.[4]

The execution of the Earl must have been the one topic of conversation in the city for many days to come; inhabitants of the district where he died and parishioners of the church where he was buried must long have remembered the happenings on the Pavement. Margaret's cousin Edward Turner must have had much to say about the manner of his death, for he would have been an eye-witness, as one of the two sheriffs of the city of York (but yielding precedence to the Sheriff of Yorkshire, since the Earl had not been condemned in the city). His fellow-sheriff, James Birkby (an attorney practising before the Council in the North) was a Protestant, and any lingering traces of the religion of Edward's father, Thomas Turner, were disappearing from his own memory.

The oppressed minority whose beliefs and actions were beginning to interest Margaret Clitherow were entering on a period of persecution which far surpassed in scope and intensity anything that had gone before. Their difficulties had been increased beyond measure by the issue in 1570 by Pope Pius V — too late to assist the Earls' rebellion, which had already failed — of a Bull excommunicating the Queen. This had repercussions so extensive, and of such a nature, as to make the survival of the Catholic Church in England, even in the diminished form it held for centuries, nothing short of a miracle. For the Pope, relying on a medieval conception of his power, declared Elizabeth deposed for heresy, and her subjects absolved from their allegiance to her. This in itself made every English and Welsh Catholic a potential traitor in the eyes of the State, and resulted in the enactment of a further series of penal laws which remained on the statute book for more than two hundred years.

That the papal Bull was an immense and tragic blunder was conceded by Pope Urban VIII (1623–44), who, urged to excommunicate the kings of France and Sweden, refused to imitate his predecessor's action, saying, *'We bewail it with tears of blood.'*[5] By the end of his reign more that two hundred and thirty English and Welsh Catholics had died, mostly by the hideous penalty reserved for treason, and the roll-call of martyrs was by no means complete.

The Parliament that met in April 1571 had made it treason to deny that Elizabeth was the lawful Queen, also to employ any Bull, writing or instrument of absolution or reconciliation with the Roman See, to absolve or reconcile another, to receive such absolution or reconciliation. . . . It was in that atmosphere that Margaret Clitherow began to make enquiries, and when, late in 1573 or early in 1574 — she was carrying another child, Anne, at the time[6] — she was reconciled with the Roman Church, she consciously took a step that laid her open to a charge of treason, the penalty for which, in the case of a woman, was burning to death.

Meanwhile, her husband was accepting responsibilities in his parish and city. Already in December 1572 he had been chosen, as one of the 'discreet and honest' parishioners of Christ Church (the popular name for the parish of Holy Trinity, King's Court), to assist the churchwardens, constables and 'sworn men' to carry out the instructions of a Commission issued by the Council in the North under its new, Puritan Lord President, the stern and effective Henry

48

Hastings, third Earl of Huntingdon. Their orders were to report without favour or affection all known or suspected Papists and especially those who refused to attend their parish church, and all who were 'fugitives and fled out of the realm for religion. . .' and 'such as do lurk and be kept secret in any house. . . .'

Unfortunately, two of the most deeply respected residents in the parish of Christ Church were well known for their fidelity to the 'old religion', and their decent fellow citizens were very loath to report them, or, indeed, any of their neighbours. These two were Dr Thomas Vavasour and his wife Dorothy.

Dr Vavasour (son of Sir Peter Vavasour of Spaldington), who had graduated from St John's College, Cambridge, shortly after the martyrdom of its founder, St John Fisher, was one of the outstanding lay Catholics of Yorkshire. During his exile in Venice in the reign of King Edward VI, he had qualified in medicine, which he practised in York on his return in the reign of Mary. He was able so learnedly to defend his religion 'against all who did impugn it, that it was reported that he would turn the whole city if he were suffered to talk'. In 1570 unknown correspondents reported to Cecil that they had been 'hunting' for Dr Vavasour for the last two years without success; in fact he had not been seen in York since just before the Earls' Rebellion. His 'chaplains', however, had been saying Mass at his house.[7]

His wife was as staunch a Catholic as he; she 'encouraged much her good and virtuous husband to be constant in the Catholic faith', for 'seeing him somewhat careful [i.e. worried]' she 'did desire him to cast away all care and fear for her and his children, and to do that constantly and nobly in God's cause which his conscience did teach and move him to do. Herewith, he . . . did take heart . . . and prepare himself, with God's grace, to suffer what persecution soever God should suffer to fall upon him.'

As Dr Vavasour was still 'so befriended' that his enemies could not find him, the discreet and honest company pledged to give information about him in 1572 could probably declare quite truthfully their ignorance of his whereabouts.

From what is known both of Mrs Vavasour, 'the chief matron and mother of all the good wives in York', and of the subterfuge employed by Margaret in order to gain instruction without her neighbours' knowledge, it is possible to reconstruct the course of events. For Mrs Vavasour, the doctor's wife, ran what can only be described as a Catholic maternity home, where 'women, their times of bearing and bringing forth their children approaching, had good and safe being, both for the time of their delivery, the christening of their children, and the recovery of their health again.'[8] And Margaret Clitherow 'procured some neighbours to feign the travail of some woman, that she might under that colour have access and abide with her ghostly Father the longer'. In other words, when the 'goodman' or priest came to Mrs Vavasour's house, she had only to send a servant round to Margaret, and the neighbours would suppose that one of the mothers known to be at Mrs Vavasour's was in labour and needed assistance.

Who it was that instructed Margaret Clitherow and eventually received her into the Church it is impossible to say, but he was almost certainly an old priest ordained under Mary, or even under Henry VIII, who had faculties to absolve those who returned to the Faith. To judge from a passage recorded during one of the interminable interrogations to which Margaret was subjected at the end of her life, she had been acquainted with Fr Henry Comberford, who was imprisoned in York from 1570 until his transfer to Hull in 1576. Archbishop Sandys in 1577 reported that the majority of the most obstinate recusants in his new diocese had been 'corrupted' by Henry Comberford. His career is therefore of some relevance to the story of Margaret Clitherow.

Henry Comberford was old enough to have experienced every stage of the English Reformation, having taken his first degree in the University of Cambridge in 1533, while the Reformation Parliament was still sitting. A native of Comberford, in the county of Staffordshire, he was possibly a nephew of Sir Anthony Fitzherbert, the great lawyer, whose sister Dorothy had married Thomas Comberford; certainly he held at least one living that belonged to this family. He was a Fellow of St John's College, and in 1543-4 he was one of the University proctors. Together with other scholars who later became staunch defenders of, and sufferers for, the papal supremacy, Comberford subscribed to the declaration against it.

In 1542, in a constitutional dispute with the new Master of the college, Henry Comberford appeared at a visitation as one of the proxies for the appellant party (mostly conservative northerners); they included Alban Langdale and Thomas Watson. (The opposition party was led by John Cheke, the greatest English classical scholar of the day, soon to be knighted and appointed tutor to Prince Edward, and also to Henry Hastings.)

The events of the reign of King Edward VI convinced Comberford that the only guarantee of stability in the Church was acknowledgement of the successor of St Peter as the Vicar of Christ on earth. As Archbishop Heath expressed it in 1559, 'By the relinquishing and forsaking of the See of Rome, we must forsake and flee . . . the unity of the Christian Church, and by leaping out of St Peter's ship, hazard ourselves to be overwhelmed and drowned in the waters of schism, sects and divisions.'

That this position was something deeper than a conviction forced upon Comberford by circumstances was to be demonstrated by the subsequent career of this 'godly, grave and wise' priest, who spent sixteen years in prison and was held responsible by Archbishop Sandys for the strength of the Catholic opposition in York after the Earls' Rebellion.

At Elizabeth's accession, Comberford was incumbent of the Fitzherbert living of Norbury, co. Derbyshire, besides being Precentor of Lichfield Cathedral. His friend Alban Langdale held at this time, among other posts, the Chancellorship of Lichfield, while Thomas Watson was Bishop of Lincoln. In 1559 these three men were among the not inconsiderable number of clergy who suffered deprivation on refusal to subscribe to the oaths of Supremacy and Uniformity. Though at first they were treated with comparative lenience, two of the three were to spend many years in prison, Watson being the last member of the old English hierarchy to die in England. (He, incidentally, was to declare that in spite of the papal Bull of 1570, he continued to recognize Elizabeth as his lawful sovereign.[9]) Alban Langdale, however, was allowed to live for years under bond as chaplain to Viscount Montague in Sussex. His secretary there was none other than *John Clitherow's brother William*, who wrote out for him — or possibly for another Langdale — a notorious pamphlet permitting attendance at the services of the established church, a fact that was to make him unpopular as a late student for the priesthood at Rheims in 1580-1. (Whether Margaret Clitherow ever so much as met this brother-in-law is unknown. The author of the pamphlet she would not have approved of, but Alban Langdale's former association with Henry Comberford is of some interest, and there may have been links here that have gone unrecorded. Did William Clitherow, for instance, bring letters to York from Alban Langdale to the imprisoned Comberford?)

Comberford, having disobeyed the royal proclamation of 27 December 1558 by preaching what described as a 'lewd' sermon in Lichfield Cathedral, was reported to the Privy Council by the Bailiffs and Burgesses of the city. Considered to be learned but wilful, for a time he was confined to the county of Suffolk, with liberty to travel twice a year into Staffordshire. After the Earls' Rebellion, however, in November 1570, he was captured in the house of the Dowager Countess of Northumberland in Sheffield, and sent to the upper Sheriffs' Kidcote on Ouse Bridge, York, whence he 'exercised a modest apostolate, sending his servant out with messages and papers and receiving a number of visitors'.[10]

It was to this prison that William Tesimond was re-committed in November 1572 after his appearance before the High Commission; it seems likely that his instinctive dislike of the new church service had been strengthened by instruction from Fr Comberford. William Tesimond was related to the wife of John Clitherow's cousin John Weddell; perhaps

Margaret, whose cousin Edward shared responsibility for this prison as sheriff in 1572, visited Tesimond there and so met Fr Comberford?

If, in 1586, a York butcher's wife, an 'unlearned' woman, is found discussing the Fathers of the Church with her adversaries, it may well be that she had been instructed and received into the Church by Fr Henry Comberford, Master of Arts and Bachelor of Divinity. He was not, however, her only source of instruction; Fr Mush relates a strange story showing to what lengths Margaret would go to obtain it.

'When she was invited with her neighbours to some marriage or banquet in the country, she would devise twenty means to serve God that day more than any other at home; for she would take horse with the rest, and after that she had ridden a mile out of the city, one should be there ready provided to go in her stead, and all that day she would remain in some place nigh hand, where she might quietly serve God, and learn of her ghostly Father some part of her Christian duty as her heart most desired, and at night return home again with the rest as though she had been a-feasting all the day long.' (How this complicated arrangement was made and carried out without discovery is not explained; but it is possible that Margaret and her 'double' wore the silken face-masks — Shakespeare's 'sun-expelling mask' — which came into fashion in 1572.) This exploit must have taken place some years before Margaret's first imprisonment in 1577; it is the only glimpse we have of the life-style of her early years. By this time she was consciously acting a part, and a dangerous one. Soon after her conversion she was still hot-headed, fully resolved 'rather to forsake husband, life and all, than to return again to her damnable state'. This 'dare-devil' element in her was to be slowly tempered by suffering.

Margaret was not content with merely finding the true Church of Christ and becoming a member of it; she experienced a complete conversion of heart. She had seen not only the Church founded by Christ, now suffering and hidden, she had seen herself, a soul baptized indeed, but lacking guidance, with faults hitherto unsuspected and bad habits unchecked. She needed God's grace, not only to deliver her 'from error in faith' but also from 'ungracious affections of the will', impulses devoid of grace. She set herself to overcome her faults of character, and 'laboured to lay a sure foundation of true and unfeigned humility'.

Twelve years later Fr Mush noted her true love of God as reflected in three ways. 'First, that she had every day a hearty sorrow and humble repentance for her youth spent out of Christ's Catholic Church, in vain follies and schism, which daily exercise wrought in her a continual sorrow, to recompense those years, and with her whole strength by God's grace to honour him, as she had dishonoured him before.' The conviction that she had not remembered her Creator in the days of her youth but had frittered away much of her time in the continual round of thoughtless gaiety and worldly pleasures common to her class clearly haunted her for the rest of her life. 'From the beginning of her conversion' she had so abandoned worldly pleasures 'that they molested her not once in the whole year'. She felt a loathsomeness for 'her sinful and unprofitable life in the world, as unworthy of any benefits from God'. She had 'a contempt and hatred of the world and of all the vanities and pleasures therein . . . accounting them all temptations and baits to deceive Christian souls'.

The second mark of her love of God was her 'vehement desire' to convert others, 'that God might be glorified in all his people'. Thirdly, she was resolved to do nothing, however slight, that she thought was offensive to God.

When once her friends and relations — and, first, of course, her husband (who was serving as one of the six chamberlains of the city for the year 1574) — realised that she had become a Catholic and a recusant, her personal troubles began. 'She passed not in any company without her crosses.' Her stepfather, always aware of her as the future owner of the house he lived in, must have exerted all his charm and persuasive powers upon her (as he was to do at the end, when he 'by all flattery allured her' to disobey her conscience), with increasing annoyance and frustration at her stubbornness. Her mother must have begged her to withdraw from so dangerous a situation, which was making things difficult and unpleasant, not only for John but for dear Henry, who was so ambitious and hard-working. Her younger brother, the draper George Middleton, had his own way of expressing his disapproval: between 1575 and 1585 he fathered eight children, four of whom were daughters, but not one of the four was given the name of Margaret. (Her elder brother, Thomas, a tile- and brick-maker, as a member of a handicraft occupation, would be rather despised by her wealthier relations. He plays no part in her story, and possibly died in the fifteen-eighties.) Her sister's son, William Hutchinson, who had entered the prestigious craft of the goldsmith and had acquired his freedom in 1572, probably had little contact with his aunt, the recusant wife of a butcher. Her cousin Anne Jackson, whose friends must now have been found among the families of the staff of the Council of the North, must have felt ashamed of her, too, and her husband, the attorney, must have argued with her and stressed the dreadful legal consequences to which her wicked folly might expose her. She must have been an embarrassment to Anne's brother, the former weaver, Edward Turner, who, in 1578, as a member of the Twenty-Four, was among the notabilities of York named in a Commission from the Queen and the Privy Council for the seeking out of 'massing or popish priests'. (Thomas Jackson, who had been sheriff in 1574, was also named in this Commission.[11])

As for Margaret's more distant cousin, Edward Turner the examining-clerk (increasingly close to that Secretary Eynns who had found his presence so essential), he was pleased enough to avail himself of Henry May's assistance and ingenuity when investing in land, but would prefer not to acknowledge his kinship with Henry's notorious stepdaughter. Even Edward Turner's sister, Alice Hall, and his daughter, Katherine Blenkarne, would eventually take sides against her: by 1585, the widowed Alice Hall was a servant, probably a lady's maid, to Mrs Elizabeth Eynns, widow of the Council's Secretary—she bequeathed her a gown—

and Katherine Blenkarne was also so closely connected with her household as to be a witness to the codicil of her will.[12] Margaret must have become ever more isolated from the people among whom she had grown up, and who had loved her once.

VII

Imprisonment

MARGARET CLITHEROW was by no means the only woman in York to be disturbing her family in this way; it is those strands of inter-relationship and professional interest leading into the Council in the North that make her case particularly unusual at this stage.

Mrs. Vavasour was among the first women to appear before the High Commission for Causes Ecclesiastical, and remained one of the most consistent. Another was a butcher's wife (who was also a butcher's daughter), Janet Geldard, wife of Percival Geldard, of Christ Church parish, who was reported as a recusant earlier than Margaret Clitherow, converted her husband, and is said to have died in prison during the 1580s. (Was she an influence upon Margaret at their gossiping and feasting, or had Margaret, reported to have used these occasions for apostolic purposes, influenced her?) On 12 December 1575, Janet Geldard, together with Frances, wife of George Hall, draper, and Isabel, wife of Peter Porter, tailor, appeared before the High Commission, refused to go to church and were imprisoned, Janet in York Castle and the others in the Kidcote. Imprisonment was reserved for those recusants who appeared most likely to influence others; the most dangerous were sent to the Castle.

In 1576 Lord President Huntingdon, under instructions from the Privy Council, began a concentrated attack upon York recusants; he insisted that the Corporation, still largely reluctant, should order the churchwardens to make searching and detailed inquiries into church attendance. The names of Janet Geldard and Frances Hall were included again in a list of recusants in Christ Church parish on 6 June 1576, together with 'the wife of John Clitherow'.[1] Margaret's recusancy had probably been overlooked previously on account of further pregnancies.

Dorothy Vavasour and Isabel Porter also appear in this list of twenty-three women and ten men from twelve city parishes. For the first time William Branton (son of Stephen) and his wife appear, and the wife and family of William Tesimond.

On 23 November 1576 the name of Margaret Clitherow was included in a list sent by the Corporation to the Council in the North, as one who 'cometh not to the church, for what cause we cannot learn, for she is now great with child, and could not come before us'.[2]

On 2 August 1577 both Margaret and her husband appeared before Edwin Sandys, Archbishop of York, Matthew Hutton, Dean, William Palmer, Chancellor of York Minster, and other Commissioners;[3] this was the occasion described by Fr Mush as Margaret's 'first public conflict with heretics', after which, 'she never feared nor once shrunk at any worldly affliction or pain sustained for the Catholic faith and her conscience'. John, asked whether he would undertake to bring his wife to church, said that he would advise her to the best of his ability to go to church, but he refused to pay the forfeits; whereupon he was committed to the Kidcote prison, together with several other husbands in like case. Margaret was sent to the Castle, in company with Anne Weddell (wife of John Weddell, junior, cousin to John Clitherow), Isabel Porter, Anne Cooke (wife of Ambrose Cooke, saddler, and daughter of Stephen Branton), Janet Geldard and Margaret Tailor (wife of Thomas Tailor, a tailor).

The husbands were released after three days, through the mediation of the Archbishop. On 29 October they appeared before the High Commission again, and the question of their payment of the fines was left for the Corporation to decide. On 18 November the High Commission gave permission for them to visit their wives. (On this occasion it was 'appointed that Geldard's wife be separate from the rest', and the others, Mistresses Weddell, Clitherow, Porter and Tailor, be put in a chamber together.)

On 27 January 1578 the husbands appeared once more before the Commission, and on 9 February all the women except Anne Cooke were released upon bonds to return to the Castle again on Tuesday after Low Sunday (8 April), and not to confer with disobedient persons. On 8 April further bonds were taken for the wives to return on 26 June and meanwhile not to leave their houses except to go to church. The husbands were to pay two shillings for every Sunday and holy day on which their wives missed church.

In June 1578, first Anne Weddell, and then Margaret Clitherow were, for 'special causes', unstated, excused from returning to prison; in Margaret's case the dispensation was to last until the Monday after Michaelmas (6 October), her husband seeing to her good behaviour and paying the fines for her. On 6 October both appeared; John paid thirty shillings in fines and took a new bond. On 8 April 1579 John was ordered once more to pay the fine.[4]

Among the Catholics in the Castle shortly before Margaret's first period of imprisonment was the saddler, William Tesimond, transferred from the Kidcote. He had told the High Commission in 1572 of 'his misliking the order of the service . . . for that sacrifice is not offered in the same for the sins of the quick and the dead'. In 1573 he told them he 'was not satisfied in conscience to communicate', and that the Roman Church 'was and still is' the Church of Christ. His treasured possession, the hairs of the beard of the good Earl of Northumberland, had been taken from him, and he had sat in the stocks with Thomas Bell in the frost and snow of a north-country winter. He had again been transferred, this time to one of the Hull prisons, together with Thomas Oldcorne, a poor tiler, of St Sampson's parish, who was to spend many years there. (Oldcorne's wife Alice, equally constant, died a martyr in chains in the Kidcote in 1587. His servant Anne Godfrey was a recusant too in 1576.[5])

The history of William Tesimond (whose relative, Robert

Tesimond, was a close neighbour of the Clitherows) was later to cause Margaret considerable anguish.

A recusant wife was a great disadvantage to a tradesman, especially to one like John Clitherow, who was frequently absent from York. When Margaret was in prison, he lost his wife and the manageress of his shop, he lost a great deal of valuable time attending the court, and, whether she were in or out of prison, he lost considerable sums of money. (A sympathetic court was, however, sometimes kind to him; when he entered a new bond on 6 October 1578 'it was decreed that no advantage should be taken against him for his other bonds'.[6])

Clearly there were frequent arguments between husband and wife on the subject of religion, unprofitable on both sides. Yet they took place in an atmosphere of love: 'he would ever report that he could wish no better wife than she was, except only for two great faults, as he thought, and those were, because she fasted too much, and would not go with him to the church'. As for Margaret, she was to say, 'Know you that I love him next unto God in this world.'

The prisoners at York Castle were housed not in Clifford's Tower but in a more modern building within the castle enclosure, near the great stone gate that faced Fishergate. On the far side of the wall lay the moat formed by the river Foss as it ran down to the Ouse, making the prison 'somewhat noisome'. Later descriptions of searches enable a reconstruction of the building to be made: it seems to have consisted of two wings, several storeys high, joined no doubt by the keeper's house. The two wings looked on to the yard and the Moot Hall, where the Assizes for the county were held.

One wing of the prison was the 'common side', where felons and others awaiting trial for crimes were housed, while the other was occupied by recusants, of whom, by 1599, there were fifty-three. When a new prisoner was brought in or anything unusual happened, the Catholics came to their windows.

The recusants' wing was near the 'outgate', and their

rooms are described as 'little'. There are references to a kitchen and a parlour; perhaps it was here that a prisoner in 1582 groping his way in the early morning to Fr Bell's Mass knocked over a stool and roused the Keeper. There were plenty of chimneys, but no doubt fuel, like all other necessities, cost the prisoners dear. They were free to have money, clothing and bedding sent in. For most, prison life involved a constant drain of money to the gaoler for rent, fuel, laundry, food and cooking, or for the privilege of providing their own commons, fees for fetters, and bribes for their removal. The gaoler having paid for the patent of his office was obliged to recover the outlay as best he could, and his hand was ever stretched out for bribes to turn a blind eye on forbidden activities.

On 3 October 1580 Margaret appeared once more before the High Commission, refused to take an oath or to conform, and was committed close prisoner to the Castle again;[7] here she remained until 24 April 1581, when she was released for childbirth.[8] This imprisonment robbed her of the chance of a meeting that would have given her great joy: in February 1581 Mrs Vavasour (almost certainly) entertained Saint Edmund Campion in her house in Christ Church parish.

Rules and regulations for the surer custody and restraint of the Catholic prisoners made during this period survive, but from Margaret's experience as a prisoner it is evident that in spite of his bond, the Keeper still permitted much laxity and the living of a much fuller Catholic life than was possible at home.

The prisoners were to be divided into groups, to be kept in separate places and not to mix: priests, schoolmasters and the learneder sort; gentlemen; inferior persons, 'to wit, men'; women. Special licence from the High Commission was required for any seeking access to a prisoner. A register of articles brought for the use of prisoners was to be kept. The Keeper was to provide sufficient diet, good meat and drink, well served, each prisoner to pay at the rate established for the Fleet prison in London. Letters and books intended for the prisoners or to be sent out by them, were to be censored by the Dean, the Sub-Dean, the Archbishop's Chancellor or the Chancellor of the Minster (William Palmer). The Keeper was daily to offer to accompany the prisoners to church. Once a month, the Chancellor, the Sub-Dean and two Protestant aldermen (who were Commissioners), or three of them, were to 'survey the prisoners' and see that the regulations were being observed.[9]

A woman is by nature less well adapted than a man to compulsory community life of any kind, and Margaret's first experience of it must have been a shock. Accepting it as God's will, however, she soon adjusted herself to loss of personal liberty and even to the invasion of her privacy by Protestants. At her first imprisonment, and at intervals afterwards, she was forced to listen to the arguments and attempted persuasions of the Protestant divine, Edmund Bunney, who became a familiar acquaintance. She always answered him that whatsoever the Catholic Church taught and believed, that she firmly believed.

'The spirit of God wrought so graciously in her', says Fr Mush, 'that all troubles, persecutions, and cruelty practised against her for Catholic religion and conscience' sake daily increased more and more the constancy of her faith.' Margaret accounted the prison 'a most happy and profitable school, where the servants of God (as delivered from all worldly cares and business) might learn most commodiously every Christian virtue. And surely this fruit she reaped of it at all times, that there she made her provision, and heaped together such good store of virtues as might serve her need whensoever she should be set at liberty, and drawn again into the malignant world. In this her imprisonment, therefore, she greatly deceived her enemies, which intended by such terror and violence to weaken her strength, to abate her courage, and to infringe her constancy; for every day she, growing stronger than herself, marvellously increased in fervour and charity to God and man, planted in her heart a perfect contempt of the world, and laboured principally to overcome herself in all disordered passions and inclinations of nature, that her actions and service might be acceptable in the sight of God, as she preferred his honour and will before all things.'

The first lesson she learned in her 'school' was detachment from those who were nearest and dearest to her; 'she thereby became familiar with God'. Her forcible removal from the business in which she was daily 'tossed up and down', from 'the disquietness and cares of this world' which impeded her endeavour 'all the day long to have her mind fixed on God', gave her at last an opportunity for uninterrupted prayer and meditation on spiritual things.

Margaret's second lesson arose from the simple necessity of doing housework for herself; for the first time she was without the servants to which a woman of the merchant class was accustomed. Having to face the realities of life, she found that the means of overcoming her own inclinations and reaching sanctity lay around her.

For the rest, Margaret learned by contact with her fellow prisoners, and became habituated to devotions and practices perhaps unknown to her before. Like other prisoners, she used the 'discipline' or scourge, when she could obtain her confessor's permission.

On returning home, Margaret found that she could no longer endure the 'banquets' she had formerly attended and used for apostolic purposes. In prison the Catholics fasted four days in the week, 'partly for lack of necessary victual, partly to satisfy for their former sins, partly for the greater merit, and the sooner to procure God's grace again to his afflicted Church.'

When she returned to the Castle in 1580, a well-educated gentleman, Brian Stapleton, was among the prisoners on the men's side;[10] he was to spend several years there, but eventually escaped. By 1586 he was hidden in Margaret's house and employed as tutor to her children and others. (Margaret 'prayed God that her children might have virtuous and Catholic education, which only she wished to be their portions'.)

Another person who was probably still in the Castle was

the 'gracious' Anne Lawnder, very much a kindred spirit. She was a grand-daughter of Sir John Constable of Burton Constable. 'When she was abroad' she 'had fed daintily and delicately, and had gone bravely, according to the time, and the glorious pomp of this vain world'. Coming to prison, 'she viewing the place well, and considering that it was the school of Christ, in place of her brave gown, trimly set out with fringe and lace, put on a kind of mourning weed. She now laid apart her golden coifs and shining cowls, with her gorgeous hats adorned with gold, and trussing up her fine frizzled locks, which were wont to be laid abroad for a show, she put upon her head homely attire, and used to wear a mean felt hat . . .'.[11]

One of the most painful aspects of Margaret's imprisonment was the fact that she was separated from her children. In other prisons in York, on the bridge, for example, children lived with their parents; yet Fr Mush expressly says that Margaret was separated from house, children and husband.

In general, sixteenth-century women were quite unsentimental about children. The rate of infant mortality was, in any case, so high that they had to steel themselves against the possibility of losing half their children. Anne Lawnder left seven young children to be brought up by others while she and her husband faded away in prisons in York, Hull and London, simply for this matter of conscience.

In York Castle the community of Catholics — and despite the regulations, they did form a community — was very mixed, containing both sexes, celibates and married laity, and a wide range of ages and social classes, and, most important, of religious experience. One thing they already had in common: unselfish zeal for the cause of Christ's Church. This cross-section of English Catholic society was welded together by normal religious devotions and practices, until it became 'that blessed society in the Castle'. 'Singularity', as unusual private devotions were termed, was discouraged, for in the heightening persecution Catholics became intensely aware of their solidarity in Christ.

In the Castle, Margaret progressed in the spiritual life, acquiring more docility, that 'fervent mildness' and spirit of obedience which Fr Mush was later to find in her. She began, too, to develop the delicacy of conscience that was to become an outstanding characteristic.

The actual conditions in the Castle being so lax, Mass was frequently said there by priest-prisoners, and even, on one famous occasion, sung. Confessions were heard, sometimes through holes in the wall or the floor-boards. There was opportunity for communal prayer, conversation, discussion and instruction. So valuable were these contacts between Catholics that imprisonment usually strengthened their faith and resistance. John Towneley, half-brother of the Dean of St Paul's, was thought at one time to be 'conformable', but after imprisonment in York Castle 'he was rather made worse than better,' the High Commission reported, 'by conference with persons worse affected than himself'.

It was so much easier to live a Catholic life in these conditions that more than one prisoner 'wished to die rather in prison than in any other place'. Margaret Clitherow 'thought herself not in good case that she was so often delivered out of prison, and would say that she was unworthy so high a calling'. 'I fear God saw something in me for which I was unworthy to continue among them,' she said, 'but God's blessed will be done.'

VIII

The Holy Sacrifice

THE crown of Margaret's spiritual life was her encounter with God by participation in the holy sacrifice of the Mass. English Catholics were now living at an unparalleled intensity of spiritual experience. The Protestant attack on the Mass had called forth a much greater devotion to, and understanding of, it among Catholics, and when the saying or hearing of Mass became penal offences, those who took part in it became deeply aware of their share in the redemptive suffering and sacrifice of Christ.

It was with an increased appreciation of the holy sacrifice of the Mass that Margaret returned home from her first imprisonment, in June 1578. 'After her deliverance out of prison she straightway provided place, and all things convenient, that God might be served [i.e. Mass said] in her house.'

Fr Mush, describing the search of Margaret's house in March 1586, states briefly that the priest's room 'was in the next neighbour's house'. His reference to this chamber, and to a 'privy conveyance for safety' (an escape route) which was 'without her own house' and was in fact successfully used by Fr Mush himself on this occasion, are vague, and the degree of complicity of Margaret's neighbour uncertain.

The author of the 1619 *Abstract*, who had access to other 'writings' besides the *True Report*, elaborates a little: 'knowing the persecution to be great, and the eyes of the State watchful over her, she ever kept her priest within a chamber of her neighbour's house (which she had hired for that purpose) and had made not only a passage from her own house unto that chamber, but means for the priest to escape (without coming to her house) upon the least notice of any danger. . . .'

One of the difficulties of tracing the history of ancient properties in York lies in the fact that from the sixteenth century, or even earlier, the internal arrangements were frequently altered, some houses being enlarged by the inclusion of rooms from a neighbouring house or by the demolition of walls. (To this day, the interiors of some of the Shambles houses resemble a rabbit warren.)

If Margaret planned and carried out such an addition to her husband's house, the extent of his knowledge comes into question. (A married woman could not actually 'hire' a room or make a contract, though she might, of course, make a private and unofficial agreement.) When asked at her arraignment whether John had been privy to her doings in keeping priests, she was to reply, 'God knoweth I could never yet get my husband in that good case that he were worthy to know or come in place where they were to serve God.'

The entrance to the priest's room was so well constructed that it would have remained undiscovered had not a terrified boy betrayed it. The work must have been carried out during one of John's frequent absences from home. We may wonder whether, perhaps, John was rather lame, and could not easily reach or explore some of the upper rooms of his own house.

The identity of the obliging and trustworthy neighbour is of great interest. At some time between 1574 and 1576, new tenants had moved into the houses on either side of John Clitherow's,[1] and as it happened, both were related to him. On one side there now lived his sister Millicent, who was married to another butcher, William Calvert;[2] on the other side was Michael Mudd, also a butcher (either brother or uncle to John's first wife, Matilda Mudd) and his wife Ellen.

It seems that in the period between her first and second

imprisonments, Margaret's apostolic activities bore fruit among both these families. She 'had a special care' over 'her neighbours and citizens . . . if they were schismatics, to reduce them again to the Catholic unity; if they were heretics, and she had any hope of their conversion, or through some familiar acquaintance with them doubted not of their secrecy, to have them instructed in the true faith'. 'And in this *her perfect charity toward God* she let no occasion slip, no opportunity escape, to draw all with whom she might safely deal, to their dutiful and sincere obedience toward God.'

Unfortunately, during a second great sweep of recusants made in 1580 by the High Commission, both these families conformed, as did many others, to Margaret's great grief and 'anguish of mind'.

On 3 October 1580 a large number of one-time recusants appeared before the High Commission; Millicent, wife of William Calvert, proved she was continuing her conformity, while Michael Mudd took bond for himself and his wife to conform. (Neither surname occurs again in the lists of recusants.) It was on this day that Margaret Clitherow was committed for the second time to the Castle.[3]

The priest's room in Margaret's house may already have been in use by 15 August 1578 (the Feast of the Assumption), for she was not among the Catholics caught preparing to hear Mass that day in Mrs Vavasour's house.

When once Margaret had a suitable room, she provided great quantities of vestments, linen, vessels and plate, from the ample allowance John gave her. Fr Mush tells us,

'Her most care, thought, and study was to have God catholicly served, and by all means his truth known, and him honoured.' 'In all her affairs this was the chief that she cared for, to the which as to the end of Christian life, all her other actions were referred. Fervour overcame all fear, and her inflamed zeal to God's service consumed all worldly terrors.' 'She would ever say: "I will not be afraid to serve God, and do well. This is a time of war and trial in God's Church, and therefore if I cannot do my duty without peril and dangers, yet by God's grace I will not be slacker for them. If God's priests dare venture themselves to my house, I will never refuse them." ' '

Margaret spent a further six months in her 'school' of prison before release on 24 April 1581, for childbirth. Perhaps she had already learned 'to read English and written hand'; it was in prison that she had leisure and opportunity to do so. From 1582 she was able to read Dr Gregory Martin's translation of the New Testament into English (the 'Rheims/Douai' Catholic annotated version). Fr Mush tells us that the other reading she 'most delighted' in was 'Kempis of *The Following of Christ*, Perin's *Exercise*, and such like spiritual books'.

Imagine Margaret sitting by her chamber window, ignoring the comings and goings in the Castle yard below, as she opens the precious volume to which her new accomplishment has given her the key! 'Of the Imitation or Following of Christ,' she reads, 'and of the despising of all vanities of the world. "He that followeth me," sayeth Christ our Saviour, "walketh not in darkness, but he shall have the light of life." These be the words of our Lord Jesus Christ, whereby we be admonished and warned, that we shall follow his teachings and his manner of living, if we will truly be illumined and be delivered from all blindness of heart. . . . If we will have the true understanding of Christ's Gospels, we must study to conform our life to his life as nigh as we can. . . . '

William Perin's *Spiritual exercises* were based on those of St Ignatius Loyola, which were contributing so much to the astonishing renewal of Christian life and spirituality throughout Europe and into the mission field. Fr Perin puts before his exercitants an ideal of mortification and detachment 'from all creatures, both in affection and also in understanding or mind, yea from thine own self' in order to attain perfect union with God. In very many points the life of St Margaret Clitherow as described by Fr Mush could be used to illustrate Fr Perin's precepts, so faithfully did she set herself to follow them. The horrifying detachment from her worldly friends and relatives, forced upon her by the cruel

circumstances of the time, must have been lifted to a supernatural plane by the study of this work. She comforted
herself for the opposition of her relatives and the even more
painful persecution she continually suffered at the hands of
jealous and disgruntled Catholics indebted to her for many
favours and benefits, by recalling 'the example of Abel and
Joseph, which were not persecuted by strangers, but by their
own brethren', and 'the example of Christ himself, which
was betrayed . . . by his own apostle, Judas.'

The inability of Catholics to train for the priesthood in
their own country had for several years driven them into
colleges on the Continent. Seeing the great need for English
colleges, Dr William Allen, an Oxford exile, had founded a
seminary at Douai in 1568, and in 1576 another English
college was founded in Rome. In 1574 priests trained at
Douai began to re-enter England to administer the sacraments and to strengthen the resistance of Catholics to the
almost overwhelming temptation to conform.

In 1580 the Jesuit mission to England began; the visit of Fr
Edmund Campion, S.J., to Mrs Vavasour's house would
have been a stage of his tour of the North for missionary
purposes.

By the time that Margaret was released from prison, in
April 1581, Parliament, driven by fear of the seminary
priests and Jesuits (and also reacting to the papally-spon-
sored expedition sent to Ireland in July 1579), had passed a
new and severe Act 'to retain the Queen's Majesty's subjects
in their due obedience'. It clarified the earlier law, providing
that any person reconciling another to the See of Rome, and
any person reconciled, should be punished as a traitor;
saying Mass was to be punished by a fine of 200 marks, and
hearing it, by a fine of 100 marks, with, in each case, a year's
imprisonment; absence from church was henceforth to incur
a fine of *£20 a month*; if continued for a year, two sureties of
£200 each were to be given for future good behaviour. All
schoolmasters were to be licensed, or to suffer a year's
imprisonment, and persons employing them to be fined £10

a month. The principle of the informer, which may be traced back to the reign of Henry VIII, was now introduced into the legislation, which laid down that he was entitled to one-third of the recusancy fines.

The Catholic laity, upon whose loyalty and material support the seminary priests were entirely dependent, were continually harassed. 'Officers, sergeants, pursuivants, factors, favourites and intelligencers, in every county and shire' were ready to spy upon, report and arrest Catholics and to search their houses. Catholics became the prey of every petty criminal, and of apostates from their own ranks as well.

It was just at this time that Henry May was coming forward in York as one of the Twenty-Four most eager to assist the Council and the High Commission in their efforts to extirpate recusancy. On 12 January 1581, when a special jury of twenty York aldermen and gentlemen produced before the High Commission a supplemental return of recusants (containing twenty-five new names), the first 'gentleman' listed as responsible was Henry May.[4] (In 1578 the Privy Council had ordered all innholders to keep a register not only of their guests' names and the length of their stay, but of 'the intention of their journey, from what place they come,' and their stated destination.[5] Henceforth the innkeeper was an unofficial servant of the State.)

On 1 March 1581 Henry May was elected Alderman to fill a vacancy, and became a Justice of the Peace. (Under the new Act, the courts of Quarter Sessions were empowered to deal with recusancy business; this relieved the High Commission of much work.)

In July 1581 Edmund Campion was caught in Berkshire, brought to the Tower, and tortured. While on the rack, he was plied with questions, including the names of his hosts. Delirious with pain, he either gave certain names or acknowledged them when they were put to him.[6]

The Privy Council, meeting on 4 August, instructed the Earl of Huntingdon to search the houses of those with whom

Campion had stayed.[7] On 15 August, the Feast of the Assumption and the third anniversary of the previous search, Mrs Vavasour's house was raided again.

On this occasion, the spirit of the searchers was more deeply antagonistic. They found the priest, William Wilkinson, 'an old man', evidently a Marian priest, saying Mass, and brought him 'through the streets with the vestment upon him, and two wax tapers carried before him, being mocked and spitted upon with vagabonds; the rest of his company following next after, with a great troop following them.'

Eleven lay people arrested were imprisoned for many years, some until their deaths. Mrs Vavasour, who had evaded imprisonment on the former occasion 'by favour and intercession of friends', spent the rest of her life in the prison called the New Counter on Ouse Bridge. The horror of Margaret Clitherow may be imagined when she learned that one of the Aldermen who had assisted in this raid was her stepfather.[8]

Mrs Vavasour's house had been accounted the principal Mass-centre in York, 'a house of refuge for all afflicted Catholics, of what state, degree or calling soever, resorting thither. There God's priests, wandering in uncertain places for fear of imminent danger, had harbour and the best entertainment that she could make them. There gentlemen and poor men too, so that they were honest and Catholics, were well accepted. . . . All good Catholics resorting thither had free access, with her good will, unto divine service and sacraments.'[9]

Greater responsibility for provision of the Mass now fell upon Margaret. Clearly, if her house were to be a safe refuge for priests, she would have to take very great care that neither Henry May nor his wife, her own mother, should enter it at inconvenient times. (The 'searchers' or inspectors of the Butchers' Company had a right to enter her house as well, and this was another danger to be considered. There was even a proviso in the lease of the property, for inspection by agents of the Dean and Chapter.)

Margaret already had the one room 'whereunto she might resort at any time, without sight or knowledge of any neighbours. In this she served God every day in quiet and calm times, with her children and others'. She now prepared a second room, 'distant a little from her own house, secret and unknown to any but such as she knew to be faithful and discreet, whereunto she could not daily resort without suspicion, nor at any time without the sight of her neighbours. This place she prepared for more troublesome and dangerous times, that God might be served there when her own was not thought to be safe, although she could not have access to it every day as she desired.'

Fr Mush asked her once 'why she would make that provision from her house, since she herself could not resort thither to serve God, not past once or twice in the week. "Well," said she, "my heart is with you, and I trust you remember me when I am toiling in the world. And though I cannot come as I desire, yet it doth me good and much comforteth me that I know I have you here, and that God is any way served by my means." '

IX

The Martyred Priests

THOSE troublesome and dangerous times soon arrived. The authorities at every level from the judges down to the parish constables, assisted by pursuivants and by spies, official and unofficial, began to carry out the provisions of the new Act. More than a year passed before the wave of intensified persecution reached the north of England, but between July 1581 and May 1582 eleven seminary priests and Jesuits were hanged, drawn and quartered in London, and one in Chelmsford.

The persecution stirred depths in the English soul which men and women in the easygoing days before the Reformation had hardly known, arousing a response not unaffected by the old devotion to the Sacred Passion of Christ. Moreover, the need for corporate penance for the laxity of the Middle Ages was now generally recognised; it had in fact been publicly acknowledged as early as 1523 when the papal legate declared before the German princes at Nuremberg: 'We freely acknowledge that God has allowed this chastisement [i.e. the Lutheran mass-apostasy] to come upon his Church because of the sins of men and especially because of the sins of priests and prelates.' Fr Mush's comment on the English martyrs was that the country was suffering 'God's heavy indignation for the punishment of the dissoluteness and iniquity as well in the Catholic clergy as laity'. Even the death of Saint Edmund Campion was received in this spirit: 'although,' says a contemporary writer, 'we lost the chief pearl of Christendom, yet it is well, for all men are of opinion that the offences and negligences of our predecessors and forefathers were so great, and our own sins so many, as they must needs be redeemed by the blood of the martyrs'.

St Paul had rejoiced in his sufferings for the faithful, and declared that he filled up in his flesh 'those things that are wanting of the sufferings of Christ . . . for his body, which is the church' (Col. 1. 24); so every martyr was believed to be 'partaking in his sufferings' (cf. 1 Peter 4.13). Their sufferings took all their value from those of Jesus Christ, for from his sacrifice 'all martyrdom took its origin'. Passing through 'the strait hole of a violent end' the martyrs entered at once into the glory for which others must wait. 'Death comes,' said St Cyprian in the third century, 'but everlasting life follows; we are destroyed and lose the world, but we are renewed and gain Paradise; the life of time is ended, the life of eternity begins. . . . How swift is the passage into happiness . . .!' The death of the martyrs was meaningful, significant, fruitful; 'the blood of Christians is the seed of the Church'.

Unwittingly the level-headed, worldly men at the centre of government had created the circumstances in which that new spirit which the Church had needed could blossom into deathless beauty. The seminary priests and Jesuits faced the hideous penalty with an unconquerable gaiety, not merely courage, constancy, steadfastness, but a supernatural joy which aroused fear and then anger and hatred in their enemies. This light-hearted happiness, the ability to crack jokes when the fetters were put on, the joy that drew tears even from Puritan gaolers, is the characteristic of the martyrs of the Elizabethan era.

It was not Death with which the martyrs were in love, but Life. The interior source of their gaiety was the acceptance of martyrdom as the consummation of a spiritual espousal. The Church had for many centuries interpreted the Canticle of Canticles (the Song of Songs) as the relation of the soul with Christ, culminating in union. From St Thomas More onwards the persecuted English Catholics thought of martyrdom in terms of marriage.

A constant stream of seminary priests began to pass through Margaret's house. They kept on the move continually to avoid arrest, spending a short time at one house before passing on to another. There were apparently two or three priests at a time based on York and serving the country districts round about, but until 1584–5, after Fr John Mush's arrival in England, there seems to have been little attempt at organisation.

Fr Mush tells us that almost all the priests who were captured and martyred in York in 1582–3 had been Margaret Clitherow's own confessors and spiritual directors. She was at home when the first three were arrested, tried and executed, and in the same prison with the next two when they were taken out to die. She had need of all the detachment from other persons that she had learned and practised.

Fr William Lacey had been well known in York some twenty years before, when, as a layman, he held an official position. He had been forced to become a fugitive with his wife and family, continually moving about the country to avoid arrest for recusancy. On the death of his wife he went to Rheims and was ordained in Rome after a brief training. Returning to England in May 1581, he carried on a very successful apostolate. He was arrested at York Castle in July 1582, in unusual circumstances, for he had entered it with Fr William Hart and Fr Thomas Bell, before daybreak, to assist at a High Mass *sung* by Fr Bell in fulfilment of a vow and in thanksgiving to God for his earlier liberation after years of suffering in that prison.

Fr Richard Kirkman, who had been on the English mission since 1579, was arrested near Wakefield three weeks later and brought straight to the York Assizes to be tried and condemned with Fr Lacey. The court was so crowded with Catholics on this occasion that the judges 'were forced to make room for themselves like ushers'.

Both priests died on 22 August 1582. Each heard the other's confession as, lying on the hurdle together, they were dragged over Ouse Bridge and up Micklegate, through the

Bar and out to the Tyburn on the Knavesmire. Neither priest was allowed to address the vast crowd for long.

A week later the people of York were astonished to see James Thompson, a person well known in the city, being escorted through the streets loaded with double irons, on his way to the Castle. They were equally surprised to learn that during a year's absence he had been ordained priest at Rheims. He had been arrested on the very day of the trial of Fr Lacey, in a house in St Olave's parish belonging to William Branton, who was then a prisoner on Ouse Bridge. Fr Thompson was now being removed to the Castle from another prison, where he could no longer pay the gaoler's fees.

Fr Thompson was tried by the Council, who had power to try a very wide range of cases, including treason and felony; at his condemnation on 25 November, he was transported with joy. He was hanged on 28 November at the Knavesmire in the company of criminals, some of whom he had converted, and his body was buried with theirs under the gallows. As he swung at the point of death, he was seen, to the great astonishment of the spectators, distinctly to form the sign of the cross upon his breast.

Undeterred by the fate of their companions, the remaining priests continued to minister in secret to their scattered flocks. The Christmas season placed a great physical strain upon them as they moved from house to house hearing confessions, saying Mass and giving holy communion. Fr William Hart, the priest who perhaps more than any other influenced Margaret Clitherow in both life and death, was so busy at Christmas 1582 that for five nights he was able to take only two hours' sleep.

On Christmas Day he said Mass at the house of William Hutton, in the parish of Christ Church (of which, ten years earlier, Hutton had been churchwarden. The house was still available to priests although Hutton was in prison.) That night Fr Hart lay in his lodgings, in a deep sleep of exhaustion. Suddenly he was surrounded by men brought by an apostate who had betrayed him; he was roused, taken the next morning to the Earl of Huntingdon, and then imprisoned to await trial.

Fr Hart was a scholar, a graduate of Lincoln College, Oxford, who had worked on the Yorkshire mission for the last eighteen months with such success that he was known as the Apostle of Yorkshire. During the weeks of his imprisonment in the Castle after his arrest, he was twice brought out for disputations, once with the Dean, Matthew Hutton, when he was taken through the streets in chains, and later in the presence of the Council, when his opponents were Edmund Bunney and the Chancellor, William Palmer.

On 8 March 1583, Margaret Clitherow (who, though notoriously a Catholic, had not been caught attending the Mass of any of these priests) was arraigned at Quarter Sessions on recusancy charges; she pleaded 'Not guilty' and was committed to the Castle for the third time. The names of the special jury empanelled to try her (and an apothecary, John Wright) have survived: Francis Bayne, foreman; Percival Brooke, Thomas Waller, William Beckwith, Robert Ketland, John Pinder, George Kitching, William Young, William Wood, William Gilming, George Tirry and Robert Watter.[1] (Beckwith, Ketland, Wood and Watter had been members of a previous jury before whom she and others had appeared on 3 August 1582, when she had been convicted of recusancy.[2])

At the Lent Assizes, Fr Hart was found guilty of treason. He denied the charge. 'I did not leave England with any intention of practising treason against my sovereign or my beloved country,' he explained, 'but merely that, like a good citizen, I might apply myself to study and to the practice of virtue, so that I might be able to help you and your children to attain eternal happiness. . . . I took holy orders (to which I perceived myself called by a divine vocation) to the end that, renouncing the world, I might be more at liberty to serve my Maker . . . Everywhere I have been, I have tried, as far as I could, to instruct the ignorant . . . I have also fed them with heavenly food, in order that being confirmed in good, they might strive to keep their consciences pure, and by their pious and religious life stop the mouths of those who calumniate us.'

The verdict against him was received with great indignation in court, many of the bystanders following the condemned man back to prison; and here the most apt of his pupils, Margaret Clitherow, awaited his return.

Fr Hart was executed on 15 March 1583. On the very scaffold he said, 'I have ever prayed for the safety of the Queen, and the good estate of the kingdom, and I wish her all that I, even at this moment, can desire for the salvation of my own soul. . . . I freely acknowledge her as my sovereign, and am ready to obey her promptly and gladly in everything which is permitted by the Catholic Church.'

About ten days later, Fr Richard Thirkeld was arrested in one of the prisons on Ouse Bridge by one of the four sheriff's sergeants. Fr Thirkeld, formerly a student at Queen's College, Oxford, had been ordained with Fr Kirkman, and like him had been on the English mission, chiefly in Yorkshire, since 1579. He was as holy as he was learned. For eight years he had prayed for martyrdom.

The arrest of Fr Thirkeld brought commotion into the parish of Christ Church. Two keys had been found upon him, which were identified by the locksmith who had made them. The sheriffs and aldermen—was Alderman May among them?—in the course of searching 'divers places for his chamber and chest' also searched William Hutton's house. Here they found 'a secret place with a trunk full of books'—the forbidden Catholic books in English which played so important a part in the resistance movement. These were immediately taken down to the market place at the Pavement and publicly burned. All Fr Thirkeld's belongings, too, were found in the house of a poor widow. He was executed on 29 May, after trial by the Council.[3]

These priests whom Margaret Clitherow had known and reverenced, from whom she had received the sacraments, who had directed her spiritual life, whom she had served and cared for, had set the seal upon their teaching by their deaths. With the exception of Fr Hart, they remain obscure figures; little individual personality emerges from the details of their trials and deaths. But Margaret Clitherow, of whom so much more is known, holds up a mirror to their spirituality. Fr Mush compares her to 'a honey bee' collecting 'of every flower some honey, both for her own store and her neighbour's'. In her essential simplicity she took the pattern of her instructors, whose very conduct her own reflects. Of Fr Hart in particular, who wept as he said Mass, who visited Catholic prisoners daily at the risk of his life, who was remarkable for his love of his neighbour, for the success of his apostolate, and for 'his carriage and behaviour' — his personality — which was 'so winning as to make him agreeable to all', Margaret Clitherow seems a very counterpart.

Sometimes Margaret would 'with great joy remember what Father Hart, Father Thirkeld, Father Kirkman, with other martyrs and priests, used to say or do virtuously'. Her spiritual life was still further deepened by the example of her confessors' martyrdom. Her forcible detachment, too, from each individual guide and confessor brought her still closer to Jesus Christ. 'I am Jesus whom thou persecutest' were the words spoken to Saul on the road to Damascus, and from that moment, as Paul, the apostle meditated upon the Mystical Body of Christ. It was this mystical identity of Christ with his suffering servants that gave the special value to their deaths, their relics and the places of their martyrdom.

One more priest well known to Margaret must be mentioned, although she did not live to learn of his martyrdom. Fr Francis Ingleby, born about the year 1550, the fourth son of Sir William Ingleby of Ripley (Sheriff of Yorkshire in 1564), was educated at Brasenose College, Oxford, and entered the Inner Temple in 1577. He was admitted to the seminary at Rheims in 1582, ordained priest in December 1583 and sent on the English mission in April 1584. He moved about the North, and especially Yorkshire, to good effect, and was one of the two priests named as having been harboured in Margaret Clitherow's house. Arrested on suspicion in May 1586 (having been treated with a respect that did not accord with his poor dress) he was condemned by the Council and executed at York on 3 June.[4]

'After the priests had first suffered martyrdom at Knavesmire,' says Fr Mush, '. . . and by their holy blood and death had sanctified their reproachful gallows', Margaret had a great desire 'often to visit that place, for she called it her pilgrimage; and thither she would go, accompanied with two or three virtuous women.' She did this probably between August and November 1582; Fr Hart's arrest in the December and the events that led to her own imprisonment again would have increased the danger thereafter. 'This being the common place for execution for all sorts of malefactors, distant half a mile from the city of York, made the passage sometime more difficult to her, because she might not adventure thither but by night because of spies, and only at such time as her husband was from home. Her desire was great often to go thither, . . . but by reason of this wicked time, her ghostly Father thought not good to permit her so often to go as she desired.'

The road Margaret took at dead of night led over Ouse Bridge, where her friends slept fitfully in prison, and past the Tollbooth (all unaware of what was to come). Up Micklegate she went; and out through the Bar, where, years before, the head of Thomas Percy had been placed; and so at length to the Knavesmire.

'As I remember,' continues Fr Mush, 'she went barefoot to the place, and kneeling on her bare knees even under the gallows, meditated and prayed so long as her company would suffer her.'

One of Margaret's companions on her 'pilgrimage' may have been Anne Tesh, a kindred spirit who was to share a cell with her at the end of her life, and was later to receive a dreadful sentence; her husband, Edward Tesh, a lawyer, was in very serious trouble for recusancy in 1576–81, but later conformed.

82

By the death of the York martyrs Margaret Clitherow gained advocates in heaven, but she lost spiritual directors on earth. 'Her confidence was so strong in God that she never doubted but he would endue and furnish every his priest, for the time of her need, with sufficient wisdom and discretion to direct her actions as should be most to his honour and her own spiritual good.' Some priests she found more helpful than others, whose training had been very brief; Fr Mush says they were 'not of that sufficiency which was requisite for her direction in every point in her affairs'. But she followed her confessor's direction in every respect, even if she had known him as a layman a mere twelve months before, 'and did utterly forsake her own judgement and will in all her actions'. (For all that, she still had a mind of her own. After her condemnation she was told that Fr Hart had 'said it was lawful for women that had no learning to defend their cause, to go to the church'. She answered, 'Father Hart was not of your opinion, neither would he say any such thing, and, if he had said, *I would not have believed him*'.)

When a confessor with whom 'she could have been well content, were called from her by occasion of more urgent business, she would say: "For God's sake let me not be without one or other, for whosoever beareth the name or authority of a Catholic priest shall be most welcome unto me, and find me willing by God's grace to follow his direction."' (At this period 'direction' was considered absolutely essential to the spiritual life.)

Continually she prayed to God to send her a competent director. In the early summer of 1584 he sent her Fr John Mush.

X

Growth Towards Sanctity

JOHN MUSH was born in 1552, in Yorkshire. Though it is to him that we owe the gibe that Henry May was 'taken from the beggar's staff', he seems to have come himself from a poor family. According to Fr Persons, he had been 'a poor rude serving man received and educated by the Jesuits out of charity,' but Persons disliked him for the 'impracticable temper' that made him unsuited to the Society of Jesus. An unnamed spy reporting on Fr Mush later, thought he had been 'a doctor's man', probably Dr Vavasour's. As, however, Mush began his studies in Douai in March 1576, and Dr Vavasour had not dared to live openly in York since 1568, Mush can hardly have known Margaret Clitherow before his return to England in 1583, at a time when she was in prison.

After a few months at Douai, Mush was sent to Rome to be one of the first students of the new English College there. In spite of his quarrelsome disposition, he acquired a reputation for great learning, and became, it was said, 'a complete master of style in the Latin tongue' (which unfortunately has left traces in his English style). In later years he twice acted as an arbiter in the so-called 'Wisbech stirs', and in the 'Archpriest' controversy was chosen to go to Rome to present the case for the appellants. In 1587 Fr Henry Garnet said of Fr Mush, 'Difficult it is to find anyone in England who has toiled with greater zeal and charity for the salvation of souls.'[1]

John Mush was not a gentleman — he possessed extraordinary powers of invective, and exercised them in his 'plain and blunt speech' — but he had a lively intelligence, great courage, organising ability, diplomacy, and a generous appreciation of the woman to whose house he was sent for shelter and assistance. He seems to have returned to York-shire with authority to direct the secular priests,[2] and kept on the move continually.

The meeting of Fr Mush and Margaret Clitherow was a significant occasion, for Mush was to record for posterity his recollections and impressions of her character, and to edit the accounts of her arrest, arraignment, Christian witness in prison, and death.

Even had John Mush been less ready with his pen, the name of 'Margaret Clitherow, gentlewoman' would have been familiar to us from the lists of Catholic martyrs, care-fully compiled from the late sixteenth century, and the cir-cumstances of her death known from the 1588 edition of Fr Bridgewater's *Concertatio* and the engraving published in 1592 by Richard Verstegan. The frequency with which her name appears in the High Commission Act Books, and from 1582 in the records of the court of Quarter Sessions for the city of York, would have indicated the exceptional nature of her constancy; moreover, the community of Canonesses Regular of St Augustine which her daughter Anne joined in 1596 has preserved to this day the fragrance of St Margaret's memory. Nor was Anne Clitherow the only recusant mem-ber of her generation of the family. But without Fr Mush's *True Report* we should know no more of Margaret's person-ality than we do of Janet Geldard's. (Janet, who converted her husband and is thought to have died in prison, may have been equally worthy of honour, though not put to the same test as Margaret.)

Unaware of Fr Mush's particular scrutiny, Margaret con-tinued her daily routine, and he marvelled at what he found in her. It is clear that he considered her to be, apart from those 'little imperfections . . . without the which this mortal life is not possible', a saint in any case, even had martyrdom not come her way, a saintly apostle and confessor. He found in her what he calls 'fervent mildness', a tempered strength, far removed from his own character, if his intemperate expressions are any guide. Several times he shows his awareness of his own spiritual inferiority to her: 'She never came to confession to me but before her departure I was cast into some extraordinary joy of mind, and a most comfortable remorse of my own sins . . . I saw myself far off from Thee. . . .'

Fr Mush's *True Report* is a document of great human interest, compiled not only as a record of Margaret's martyrdom but even more as an account of that life of grace without which 'so rare a victory could not have been gotten'.

His purpose is to encourage his readers 'with great diligence . . . to imitate this her first martyrdom of a virtuous life', which he desires himself also to imitate. He intends to produce a solemn didactic work in the conventional style of the period, but every so often 'the fresh memory of her excellent virtues', her happy and holy personality, her recent sufferings and his own loss, as well as her glorious triumph, cause him to produce some vivid descriptive passage, or to exclaim in a felicitous or moving phrase, as when he refers to her as York's 'most glorious citizen', or as 'my blessed mother, whom I joyed so often here to have my virtuous daughter', or to 'Thy servant . . . whom here thy goodness did adorn with so rare gifts . . . that she might so victoriously enter thy triumphant city *in her bloody scarlet robe*.'

The key to his account of Margaret's character lies in the word 'imitation'. 'Surely . . . she is a pattern of virtues given to me and others to follow, who are so slack in imitating the virtues of our Saviour. . . .' The type of holiness presented in his work follows closely the spirituality of *The Imitation of Christ*. Open the *Imitation* anywhere and some illustration from the life of Margaret Clitherow will leap to mind.

Fr Mush's account of Margaret's virtues, given under different headings, is interspersed with glimpses of Margaret as he knew her. Her 'outward behaviour' was 'mild, . . . lowly and pleasant', with a 'gracious humility of voice and countenance'. She was 'of very good liking [i.e. looking very well] as though she had fared most daintily every day', in

spite of her rigorous fasting and abstinence, and her prefer-
ence for simple foods: 'her most desire was to eat rye
bread' — this was the food of the poor — 'milk, or pottage
and butter'. Writing the year after Parliament had abolished
the Wednesday fish day, Fr Mush several times contrasts
Margaret's abstemiousness with the laxity of the age. Every
Monday, Wednesday and Saturday all the year round she
abstained from meat and took only one meal, and on Friday
she both abstained and fasted even more severely. She never
started to eat before saying a private grace, and she never set
aside titbits for herself. She had grown to dislike attending
'banquets', for, she said, she 'could never but exceed her
ordinary measure, and by reason of company and by diver-
sities of meats eat more plentifully than she wished.'

She continued as far as possible the way of life she had
learned in the 'school' of prison, where she had fasted four
days in the week; this she thought was 'no less necessary for
her spiritual good in the world'.

Under the heading 'Of her humility, the foundation of all
her virtues', Fr Mush describes at some length the
characteristic whose outward manifestation was in so striking a contrast with the customs of Margaret's class. 'There
was nothing to be done in the house so base that she would
not be most ready to do or take in hand herself, and the baser
the office should be, the more unwilling would she be the
maidens [ie. maids] should do it, but rather keep it as a
necessary exercise in store for herself of her own humility.
. . . She would not disdain, as many do, more outwardly nice
than inwardly virtuous, or think much to make the fire, to
sweep the house, to wash the dishes, to void the chamber
pots, and more gross matters also, choosing rather to do
them herself, and to set her maids about sweeter business.
Although sometimes, to teach them such acts of humility,
she would acquaint also her servants and children with
doing the same.'

The performance of such tasks in prison had been one of
the ways in which she had 'laboured . . . to overcome herself
in all disordered passions and inclinations of nature', as later

her daughter Anne was to struggle with her own high-spirited nature in the novitiate at St Ursula's, Louvain.

Even in the doing of housework, a subtle pride might lurk, but Margaret had foreseen this danger, saying, 'They that think much, and are not willing to do such base things, have little regard of well-doing or knowledge of themselves.'

Between Margaret and her servants — whom, however, she did not fail to rebuke sharply when necessary — there existed a Christian friendliness. 'God forbid,' she said, 'that I should will any to do that in my house which I would not willingly do myself first.'

She had a very poor opinion of herself. 'Notwithstanding all the good she did to many, yet both in her own eyes she thought herself nobody but an unprofitable servant to God and man, laden with imperfections, and unworthy of any good, and also (as much as she could without sin and offence to God) desired heartily so to be thought of and accounted in this world: never pleasing herself in the goodness she had already, but continually striving to get that which she perceived in herself to be wanting. I have marvelled,' says Fr Mush, 'many times to see her joy and great desire she had, that either her spiritual Father or any other could advertise her of her faults and imperfections, suspecting always her own actions not only to be impure in the sight of God, but also imperfect and not worthy of the sight of men.'

Her humility was also the foundation of her general popularity with her neighbours, Protestant and 'church-Papist' as well as Catholic. 'Every one loved her, and would have ventured for her more than for themselves, thinking to have a jewel (as indeed they had a most precious Margaret[3]), so long as she dwelt among them. . . .' 'How would they run to her for help, comfort, and counsel, in their distresses, and how familiarly would she use them, and with all courtesy and friendship relieve them.'

Perhaps it was because Margaret trusted her neighbours and servants that they proved trustworthy. They all knew or suspected when she had priests in the house saying Mass, but 'her servants . . . carried that reverent love to her, that

. . . they had as great a care to conceal her secrets as if they had been her natural children'. (They probably were no more than children themselves.) Some Protestants 'would be so careful to conceal her doings and give intelligence when they learned of any danger likely to befall, as though it had been their own affairs'.

One of the few things that had power to depress Margaret was 'the trouble of God's Church, and loss of souls'. When she heard of Catholics living 'in folly' or apostatizing — falling 'from the unity of Christ's Church' — or dying outside the Church, 'she were cast thereby into some anguish of mind'. A consideration that gave a great sense of urgency to missionary efforts was the fear that all souls dying outside the Church were damned. The idea that people could hold erroneous opinions in good faith and would be judged accordingly had not been developed, for the concept of justice, human as well as divine, was still imperfectly understood. Both Catholic and Protestant believed the other to be culpably ignorant, and charity demanded that each attempt to convert the other.

The law, however, had made conversion to the Catholic faith into treason. Margaret, a Catholic convert, moved among her non-Catholic neighbours with a 'rare discretion and prudency'. 'I have known some myself,' says Fr Mush, 'to whom she hath used [i.e. with whom she has discussed] some matters of weight, as this heretical time goeth, who, after a few words, would yield to her, and say, "For God's sake do what you will, and I am content".' Sometimes, hearing that Protestants had made tactless and dangerous remarks, 'she would have gone unto them, and with one word have stopped their mouths, won their favour, and made them sure to her,' such was her ability to handle people. Those who were in a position to judge her actions said, 'they never saw the like prudency in any woman, and that they learned more wisdom by her behaviour than ever they had done by the conversation and example of men in any degree'. In fact, during the long years of her illiteracy, Margaret had made people her study.

That Margaret's non-Catholic acquaintances did truly love her and try to understand her is shown in the incident of her husband's foolish talk at a party at a neighbour's house. 'Liberal of tongue among the pots', he 'spoke such like words as these, with an oath or two: "I cannot tell," quoth he, "what Catholics are. They will fast, pray, give alms, and punish themselves more than we all, but they are of as evil disposition in other things as we"; and uttered, moreover, some slanderous words' accusing them of immorality, 'the which she hearing, and knowing none to be Catholic but herself in that company, could not abstain from vehement weeping. Her husband called her "fool", and said he meant not those words by her . . . But all her neighbours, knowing her virtue, comforted her, saying that her husband spake but merrily, and meant no such matter as he said. She answered: "I pray God forgive him", and no more. This matter troubled her all night. . . .'

In this ugly and sad episode Margaret's neighbours appear in a better light than does her husband. Perhaps John was more tipsy than Fr Mush's words would suggest.

John Clitherow, even when sober, remains a rather unsympathetic character. He could not truly claim, as he seemed to on this occasion, to be scandalized by the conduct of Catholics, for he was married to a Catholic saint. Causes for scandal did exist, but not in the home of John Clitherow. John had some admirable qualities: he trusted Margaret implicitly, did not beat her, as George Hall beat his wife for her recusancy, endured frequent summonses to answer for her, as well as her long absences in prison, and so clearly protected her that he had to be called away from the house before it could be searched. (The enormous fines that he should have paid on her account were evidently reduced or overlooked by his sympathetic friends.)

His final tribute to his wife anticipated the official pronouncement of the Holy Catholic Church. But his total indifference to principle, his concern only with the practical consequences of recusancy, show his moral incompatibility with the young wife with whom he was so unevenly yoked.

Margaret's daily routine, when her husband was away, was entirely centred upon the Holy Mass, 'the service of God'. She could not be happy without daily Mass; if for any reason she had to miss it, 'she thought herself desolate, and ever suspected that for some fault which God saw in her, she was unworthy' of it. 'She ever feared that if anything should happen to' a priest who had lodged in her house, 'others afterward would be more unwilling to come to her, and so she should remain without the service of God.'

Margaret was used to early rising, for on three days in the week 'foreign' butchers, that is, those who were not freemen, were allowed to start selling in Thursday Market at 6 a.m. in summer and 7 a.m. in winter; in order to meet this challenge, the Shambles shops would have to be open by this time. Nevertheless, Margaret would spend an hour and a half or two hours kneeling in prayer in her own room, 'meditating upon the Passion of Christ, the benefits of God bestowed upon her' and upon her own sins.

She went to confession and usually to communion also, every Wednesday and Sunday. This privilege was a remarkable tribute to her sanctity, for even the great St Teresa of Avila, her contemporary, communicated only once a week. (Yet the Council of Trent had declared itself 'fain indeed, that, *at each Mass*, the faithful who are present should communicate. . . .'[4])

In confession, Margaret revealed 'the bottom of her heart, conscience, and every corner and secret inclination', with 'care, simplicity, lowliness, and sincerity'. She had, says Fr Mush, a 'hearty contrition and sorrow for her small imperfections'.

Most mornings, Margaret was able to hear one Mass or even two, unless her husband or some business prevented her; her children, and other people, would be present, for she made the Mass available to all who would come, without question. 'Her most delight was to kneel where she might continually behold the Blessed Sacrament, and usually she chose her place next the door, behind all the rest, in the worst and the base seats, and most unseemly corner in all the

chamber'. 'In the time of her receiving the Blessed Sacrament of Christ his Body, she ever coveted to have the lowest
place, so far as she could do it without trouble and noisome-
ness [i.e. nuisance] to others, for she would not seem to any
to desire it.'

With, surely an inward pang of grief, Fr Mush remembers
her face, upturned, as she waits with closed eyes to receive
the sacred host — the face he will never see again in this life.
'Whilst she received, her lovely and gracious countenance
was washed with sweet tears trickling from her eyes. Afterward she would depart for half an hour into some close
corner, where she might familiarly enjoy the delights of her
God, whom she had brought into the secret parlour of her
heart, and all the day after she would be merry and smiling,
yet most wary to keep her senses shut, lest she should by
negligence or false security be robbed of her treasure.'

It was a grief to Margaret that 'her worldly cares' prevented her from serving God or hearing Mass 'with as much
liberty at all times as she desired'. Her household duties and
responsibilities were always there to claim her attention, and
from the moment she opened her shop windows and hung
out her joints she was 'tossed up and down in worldly
business'. She found her work in the shop 'the occasion of
many waste words, loss of time, and distraction of the mind
from God', and 'she suffered greater and oftener conflicts in
dealing in this worldly trade . . . than in all her other affairs
besides'.

Margaret very rarely had leisure for her devotions from
after Mass 'until four of the clock in the afternoon, about
which time she would shake off the world and come to
evening-song,[5] where she, praying one hour with her children about her, afterward returned again about her care of
the household until eight or nine of the clock, at which time
she used to resort to her ghostly Father's chamber to pray a
little and ask his blessing. . . . From thence, going to her
chamber, she ordinarily spent an hour at the least in prayer
and examining of her conscience.' Fr Mush, who was 'privy
to her whole heart as much as any' admits that he cannot

find words to express her desire for purity of conscience, her sensitivity to sin. 'I will therefore speak no more thereof', he says, *'Secretum meum mihi* — "The secret shall be to myself".'

But Margaret was not self-absorbed. She was extremely well balanced; her natural qualities disposed her to be both Mary and Martha, contemplative and active. From her union with God sprang her apostolate not only towards non-Catholics but even more towards those whom she frequently called 'her brethren or sisters in the Catholic Church', for whom she 'had a special care'. Though she said she 'had no learning', yet, when the need for instruction lay within her scope, she would deal with it herself. 'The young children and novices [i.e. converts] of Christ's Church she liked greatly, and would embolden and encourage them in the way of virtue, not only by her own example, but also by some familiar or sweet counsel after her best fashion.'

For Catholics suffering 'in prison, or other furnace of trial' she endeavoured 'by all comforts and means she could devise, to make their burden light, and Christ's yoke to savour sweet to them'. A thing that gave her great delight was to gather poor Catholics into her house for Mass and the sacraments, or otherwise to arrange this for them. 'How carefully she cast her charitable eye into every corner, where thy secret servants lay desolate and afflicted, to get them fed with thy heavenly food in due season, lest, for want of thy banquet, they might happen to fall from thee. How also she hath looked to their bodily needs, and procured to every one relief with discretion; with how much gladness hath she gathered together by ten or twelve thy poor Catholic people at once, and brought to pass—first to have them purified and fed with thy gracious sacraments; then their bodies refreshed with sufficient meat and drink; herself, with a marvellous gift from thee of joy and humility, ministering and waiting on them diligently, and after refection providing money for every one according to their need.'

Probably Fr Mush is here remembering one particular occasion. What a pleasant picture this is, of the group of poor, secret Catholics taking breakfast together after Mass while Margaret bustles merrily about, serving them in person!

Margaret, who had been dependent on sermons for instruction during the years of her illiteracy, and had also benefited from the eloquence of Fr Hart, has 'a marvellous desire' to hear a sermon at least once a week, and when she collected such congregations as this she commonly asked the priest to give them 'a virtuous exhortation'.

Both her intense spiritual life and her evident love of her fellow-men arose from Margaret's love of God. 'She loved him whom continually she served, and joyfully served him whom she loved above all things.' She so totally identified herself with the interests of God and of his Church that if she were wronged, as for example when her husband wronged both her and other Catholics with his slanderous talk, it was the insult to God that she felt, and the harm such people did to themselves, and not her own injury. 'I was not then, nor am I now, anything at all sorry in respect of myself,' she told her confessor on that occasion, 'for, I thank God, I have ever been a true and a chaste wife to my husband, both in thought and deed; God and mine own conscience doth witness it; but it grieveth mine heart that he should so heinously offend God by slandering Catholics and the Catholic Church, whereby I fear me he shall more hardly come to God's grace, and be a member of his Church.'

Above all, Margaret desired to make God's truth known. 'How have I wondered, good Lord,' says Fr Mush, 'to see the charitable care, large providence, continual diligence, and toil of thy servant, to bring all to thee! To make thee, her God, sweeter to them than their own lives, or all thy created pleasures; to let all know the Catholic truth, without which there was no truth at all; to allure all men to love thee, as she, by thy grace, loved thee; above all, to turn thy wrath from the persecutors, and to have thy holy Name glorified in every degree. . . .'

Indeed, the enemies of the Church were continually remembered in her prayers. She had no rancour for her persecutors, 'for they never so often practised wickedly against the Church of Christ or herself or any member of it, but she had this in her mouth: "I pray God forgive them, and grant them grace to know their error and to amend it." '

It was, unfortunately, not only from Protestants carrying out the penal laws that Margaret had to endure persecution; throughout her life as a Catholic she suffered from the spite of 'some one or other emulous Catholic', a fact which Fr Mush takes as 'an infallible sign both of her own rare virtue, and also that she was most dear to God.' She was 'assaulted, not indifferently by every Catholic . . . but by such as were bound to her by many and singular benefits, themselves of no good desert for the same, and also nothing comparable to her in any degree of virtuous life, although externally they might be thought of no small perfection. What ungracious surmises and false judgements have some in their secret hearts conceived against her!' They 'ungratefully imagined her chiefest virtues to be their most hindrance; her praise to be their discredit . . .'; whereas she herself rejoiced in the virtue of others, which gave glory to God.

'She passed not in any company without her crosses,' remarks Fr Mush, and 'she thought this the heaviest cross of all, to see them, upon some false conceit [i.e. opinion] against her, *so uncharitably offend God*.' Yet 'she kept a most pure and hearty love to them,' considering in all humility whether she had offended them 'and that something lay secret in her which might be the cause of their unquietness.' Yet 'with the most and best' Catholics 'she was rightly esteemed of an especial virtue and good life'.

Certainly the conduct of her fellow Catholics left some- thing to be desired. Many records have survived of their noble endurance of suffering for the Faith, but Fr Mush's account points to the presence of that human element from which Christian striving is never free in this life. When Margaret heard that any Catholic prisoners behaved them- selves unbecomingly, with impatience, dissension, grum- bling, selfishness, or hankering after worldly pleasure, 'she would greatly lament their case, and say: "Fie on it, that this thing should be heard of, or be at all among Catholics imprisoned for their conscience. Methinks, by this time they should have learned to overcome themselves. . . . Jesu, methinks if they considered thoroughly these things, they should be so mortified that no such trouble nor affliction could grieve them, but rather be glad of every cross for Christ's sake." ' She earnestly prayed for such people who did not appreciate the privilege of their suffering.

Only one kind of person did Margaret actually dislike: not her persecutors, but 'worldlings and lukewarm Catholics'. Even here it was not so much their persons as their 'state and company' which she 'loathed'.

She never forgot her disappointment at the falling away of a man who had been in the habit of serving Mass at her house until the ferocious legislation of 1585 was passed, which made the sheltering of priests a felony, punishable by death. Then he 'came to her, and in the way and manner of friendly advice willed her to be more careful of herself, and since that virtue and the Catholic cause was now made treason and felony, that either she would not with such danger receive any priests at all, or else very seldom; and this he added also, that it was no wisdom to admit her children and others to God's service, and that she ought not to adventure upon these things without licence of her husband. After such other like speech he departed, leaving her in some discontentment by reason of his uncharitable talk.'

Discussion of the matter with her director settled her conscience, but the man's behaviour could not be over-looked. She often showed 'great disliking towards him and said she made less account of him than she had done, and would not care how little she had to deal with such timorous Catholics'.

Despite continual trials, active persecution, calumny and daily crosses, Margaret Clitherow remained serene. Her natural gaiety was raised by grace to a state of holy joy. 'All her actions were tempered with all inward tranquillity and comfort, with discreet and honest mirth, with mild and smiling countenance.' 'Her outward behaviour, so mild, so lowly and pleasant . . . was . . . most grateful and comfortable to all.'

Fr Mush, however, saw Margaret at her happiest, for she always had 'great gladness in the company of such as were fervent in the service of God and of virtuous life', and the presence of a priest meant that she would be able to hear Mass, without which she could 'never overcome herself . . . to be merry or without heaviness'. 'So long as she had with her a ghostly Father to serve God, no time seemed wearisome . . . no trouble or sorrow could make her heavy.' 'She bare a singular reverence to priesthood in every person, giving only respect to God, whose person and authority they represent and carry, and not to any man's person or other natural qualitities in them.' (We may wonder whether she remembered her own father's example on this point.)

Her interview with the former Mass-server raised questions of conscience which Margaret felt obliged to discuss with Fr Mush. They were exactly the kind of problems with which he had been trained to deal, for they involved her relations with her non-Catholic husband. ' "May I not", said she, "receive priests and serve God as I have done, notwithstanding these new laws, without my husband's consent?" "What think you," quoth he, "in this matter?" "Truly," quoth she, "hitherto I have been desirous to serve God, and both to know and do my duty in receiving his servants, and have put my whole confidence in you, that I might safely walk by your direction without sin: and I know not how the rigour of these new statutes may alter my duty in this thing: but if you will tell me that I offend God in any point, I will not do it for all the world." "Then", quoth he, "it is your husband's most safety not to know these things unless he were resolved to serve God notwithstanding any danger; again, by his consent and licence you should not serve God at all, and *in this, your necessary duty to God, you are not any whit inferior to him*. Neither doth the cruelties of wicked laws anything change or frustrate your duty to God: and therefore, an it were lawful and a good deed before these statutes to receive God's priests, and continually to serve him in

Catholic manner, the same is still lawful and well done; yea, and more meritorious in God's sight than ever it was. Besides this," quoth he, "no man can now refuse to receive them for fear of these laws, but he must be partaker in some part and guilty of the wickedness in the law and law-makers, as by his own deed giving them their intended scope and effect, which is to banish God's priests from their sheep, and so to abolish the Catholic religion and faith out of the whole realm." At which words, she, stricken with great joy, said: "I thank you, Father. By God's grace, all priests shall be more welcome to me than ever they were, and I will do what I can to set forward God's Catholic service." . . . ' ('Hereby you may perceive,' comments Fr Mush, 'her singular love to God, from whom to be separated a short time in this life she accounted death. And yet, for the same love and obedience to him and his priests, ready for a season as it were to forego God, lest she should any way offend God.')

In spite of Fr Mush's opinion of Margaret's 'blessed peace', her service of God in all her actions 'with joy and gladness, without fretting or lumpish mind', it is possible to sense an inner tension of which he was unaware. The problem of her husband touched her at every level. She had vowed to obey him, and to the end she did so in all save the affairs of God, but the affairs of God played so large a part in her life that she was continually faced with some new conflict of duties.

John was a human soul in danger of damnation, one of those 'with whom she might safely deal' in discussing religion, a soul entrusted to her just as much as her children were, and to him she felt the same responsibility for instruction and conversion. Yet Margaret could not even make her husband interested in the Faith. He held no definite views against it which she could combat; she fought 'as one beating the air' (1 Cor. 9. 26).

John Clitherow was set on serving Mammon, on increasing his wealth whenever possible, whereas Margaret had no desire for riches; to her surplus money was a commodity to be given to those in need. (Her almsdeeds and provision for the Mass, for which she 'spared no cost', did not affect her husband's wealth, for she spent little of her allowance on herself. On the other hand, 'in selling and buying her wares she was very wary to have the worth of them . . . to satisfy her duty to her husband'.)

Poor John! He would come home sometimes wailing about cattle murrain, or about his failure to win those lengthy tithe suits in which he was involved in the ecclesiastical courts[6], and would get no sympathy at all from his other-worldly wife. On the contrary, 'she would be exceeding merry and say, "Yet [i.e. still] he hath too much, he cannot lift up his head to God for weight of his goods; I pray God he may by these casualties know God and serve him." ' Poor John! For all his wealth, he could not win over his wife with gifts, for 'worldly pleasure . . . molested her not once in the whole year'. He could not show off his pretty wife and family at church, and she did her best to refuse invitations to the 'banquets' which he enjoyed so much.

Margaret must have prayed continually for John's conversion; the scene at the party showed how very far he was from it. She had cause to remark, contemplating some of the more prosperous citizens of York, including her own husband, that 'generally, the more folks grew in wealth the further they were from God, and less disposed to do well'.

Margaret must often have wondered what the future held for her and John, and whether she might eventually be left a widow, with her children grown up. This was not unlikely in the course of nature, for John was nearing fifty and would already be accounted an old man. She did not, in that event, imagine that she would continue to run a Mass-centre in York; in any case, Catholics of her generation still clung to the faint hope that 'Catholic times' would return. Nor would Margaret Clitherow contemplate taking a second husband, which was the normal custom.

She was becoming conscious of a personal call from God to a still more intimate union with himself, a call distant and muffled and difficult to interpret. Her experience of prison life, with its paradoxical sense of freedom, had aroused in her a longing which other Catholics had felt in prison, for the monastic cell. 'I assure thee on my faith, mine own good daughter,' St Thomas More had said in the Tower to Margaret Roper, 'if it had not been for my wife and ye that be my children, I would not have failed long ere this to have closed myself in as strait a room, and straiter too.'

'I have heard her say', says Fr Mush of Margaret Clitherow, making no comment, '"if that it pleased God so to dispose, and set her at liberty from the world, she would with all her heart take upon her some religious habit, whereby she might ever serve God under obedience". And to this end (not knowing what God would do with her) she learned our Lady's Matins in Latin.'

It was not at all unusual for a widow to become a nun; it had been a common pre-Reformation custom. Margaret Clitherow, however, had in her humility quite mistaken the nature of the higher vocation of which she was becoming aware.

She had 'a marvellous desire to suffer for Christ and his truth'. 'It was her daily prayer that she might be worthy to suffer anything for God's sake.' From the very outset of her conversion, to which the suffering and martyrdom of others had impelled her, and by the circumstances of her environment, she had been gradually prepared to complete her spiritual detachment from the world by the total sacrifice of her life for Christ. Not the religious life, but martyrdom, was her vocation.

Fr Mush, convinced of her sanctity, could joke with her about the possibility, *'yet always he thought it would happen to her reward'*. '"You must prepare your neck for the rope,"' said he. '"God's will be done," said she, "but I am far unworthy of that honour."' '"I see not in myself any worthiness of martyrdom."'

101

XI

Approaching the Climax

THE events that led up to the final solution of Margaret's difficulties began in the winter of 1584, soon after her return home again from prison under bonds, clearly under house arrest once more. 'Without the knowledge of her husband,' she then sent 'her eldest son into France for virtuous education and learning, hoping one day to see him a priest, the which she most desired.' It is a comment on the strength of her faith and her detachment from purely human considerations that Margaret should be willing to part with her son Henry, who was only twelve years old, and anxious for him to receive the priesthood which could only be exercised in England at great personal danger.[1]

Her action must have taken some explaining to John. It is not at all likely that he would understand Margaret's desire 'that her children might have virtuous and Catholic education'. The most favourable supposition that can be made about John's reaction to his son Henry's passage into France for the illegal purpose of a Catholic education is that he recognized his wife's utter sincerity and her obligation to obey her own conscience in the matter.

Not long afterwards legislation was made to deal with the problem of children sent to seminaries abroad. The plot attributed to Francis Throckmorton had been exposed in the summer of 1584 and Parliament, called in November, was anxious to pass more stringent laws against Catholics. The famous Act of the year 27 Elizabeth received the royal assent in March 1585; by it Jesuits and seminary priests were commanded to leave the kingdom within forty days. Any discovered after that period would be accounted traitors merely by reason of their priesthood 'received beyond the seas'. To harbour or maintain them was made felony; the original Bill had made it treason, but the Lords had reduced the penalty.

All students in the seminaries were ordered to return within six months. Persons sending children to seminaries were to forfeit £100, and if they sent money to any already there, to incur the penalties of *Praemunire*. The consternation of John Clitherow, held responsible in law for his wife's actions, can be imagined.

During 1585 Margaret's tensions must have increased almost to breaking-point. Her husband's lease of a property in the Little Shambles, used as a stable, was coming up for renewal, and suddenly a way of escape from her perilous situation presented itself to her. She 'was in hand often with her husband to give up his shop, and to sell his wares in gross with as much gain and with less unprofitable toil', says Fr Mush, who was in the house at the time. If only the whole family could leave York, could go to live at Cornbrough, away from the spies, the searches, the fines, the imprisonments, the secrecy, the enmity, the fear! To breathe fresh air, surrounded by fields and woods, in freedom and light, peace and quiet, away from the din and stink of the streets, the blood, the cries of terrified animals, above all, from the dark shop and the tiresome, never-ending round of worldly business! How much better, too, it would be for her children, if only John would give up the retail trade and confine his business to the wholesale!

This ambition must have been a very real temptation to Margaret. No doubt, had her husband listened to her — and it would have been an action unheard-of among prosperous butchers in mid-career — the mansion at Cornbrough would have become another Mass-centre, but all those poor Catholics in York whom she was helping would have lost their opportunities to receive instruction and the sacraments.

For some time her sense of responsibility towards these people was in abeyance. Like her hankering after the religious life, this more practicable idea was the result of ten years of acute stress, which was now affecting her physically too. (More than once she was 'deceived' into thinking herself pregnant again.) She would now appreciate more keenly the state of mind in which so many of her fellow-Catholics had conformed and gone to church. But on 17 December 1585 the new lease was signed,[2] and Margaret's yearning for green pastures had to be stifled. 'May God's blessed will be done,' she would say.

The disappearance of Henry Clitherow from the city was not kept secret for long; his godfather Henry May must soon have realized he had gone. The Council in the North 'after a while, had intelligence of' the fact, 'and greatly stormed thereat, yet *lingered to deal in the matter*'. Margaret's action, intended eventually to continue the supply of priests in England, must have provoked them beyond endurance, and they must have had good reasons for their delay. It is worth while considering what these reasons may have been.

It is possible that the key to the situation lies in the position of Margaret's stepfather, Henry May, who had continued to pursue his ambition and was now within reach of the city's highest office, that of Lord Mayor. He was assiduous in his attendance at meetings of the city Council, which dealt with administrative business. (He seems to have been less interested in the judicial functions that he possessed as an alderman. He rarely sat as a Justice of the Peace at the Quarter Sessions for the city; he made an exception on the day on which Fr William Wilkinson, Mrs Vavasour and the other Catholics arrested at Mass in her house appeared in court, for he had taken part in the raid.[3])

At this important period of Henry May's life, the city of York was becoming increasingly subservient to the Council in the North. This process may be illustrated by the rise to civic office of two Council attorneys. Thomas Jackson (Henry May's 'cousin' and one-time husband of Margaret

Clitherow's cousin-german) had been admitted to the freedom of the city in 1564 as an 'innholder'; in 1570 he served as
one of the four chamberlains, and in 1574 he was one of the
sheriffs. In 1585 a civic order forbidding Council attorneys
from exercising their profession if elected aldermen was
repealed; the following year, during Henry May's
mayoralty, Jackson was elected alderman to fill a vacancy.
He was Lord Mayor in 1589; his immediate predecessor, the
very wealthy Protestant, James Birkby, another Council
attorney, was the first such person to become Lord Mayor,
and he served a second term in 1596. (In 1589, when Jackson
was Lord Mayor, one of the chamberlains was Thomas
Blenkarne,[4] the Council clerk whose marriage in 1582 to
Katherine Turner, daughter of Edward Turner the examining-clerk, had brought him into kinship with Henry May,
with Jackson himself, and, incidentally, with Margaret
Clitherow.) The governing clique of the city, already interrelated, was now being very effectively penetrated by
devoted and Protestant members of the Council staff.

This situation was to cease abruptly with the death of the
Earl of Huntingdon in December 1595; no other Council
official became Lord Mayor so long as the Council in the
North existed. This suggests that Catholics were correct in
suspecting that the Earl of Huntingdon had 'the mayors and
other officers at his disposition'. 'Diligent care is had, that in
such offices as go by election of voices . . . the President
seeketh by covert means to have them at his own
appointment.'[5]

In January 1585 one Andrew Trewe, described, probably
by Fr Mush, as a malicious and ignorant Puritan, was
elected Lord Mayor. During his year of office he would, with
the assistance of the President, be considering who might
best succeed him, dropping hints to various members of the
Common Council before they sent up nominations. In January 1586 the Common Council put forward three names, the
first of which was Henry May. He was an obvious and
deserving choice.

Unfortunately for Mr May, it was during this very year,

when he was under the President's closest scrutiny, that his wife fell ill and died. She was buried in St Martin's on 12 June 1585.[6] The house in Davygate now passed, under the terms of Thomas Middleton's will, to Jane May's daughter; her rights over it would be exercised by her husband, but everyone knew what a weak creature he was. Under the terms of this will and probably also under some settlement the rest of Jane May's wealth would now be distributed among the heirs of her first husband.

The irony of the situation was common knowledge: a large part of Henry May's inn was now the property of his notorious papist stepdaughter, who had been under house arrest for the last twelve months. She was strongly suspected of harbouring priests; if she were taken and hanged for this offence, that property would be forfeited to the State. Both the shame of such an event and its effect upon his resources would tend to deter Henry May from attempting any action against Margaret; on the other hand, were not her recusancy and the sending of her son, his godson, abroad for education, likely to impede his own advancement? Might not the Councillors think he had himself been protecting her?[7]

He had lost some of the bargaining power of money, but he had not lost his self-confidence. He whose 'table-talk' about his stepdaughter was so free after her death, would be ready to point out, during her life, the weakness of her position: would a married woman, with children, even a woman of Margaret's determination, be prepared to *die* for her faith? She had not been sufficiently frightened; that was why she had been able to withstand all the coaxing of her friends and relations, and the arguments and threats of High Commissioners and divines for so long.

We have seen Henry May, with a fortune at stake, biding his time and striking at the crucial moment, proposing marriage to Jane Middleton indecently soon after her husband's death. He had a gambler's instinct. Now he may have felt confident that if Margaret could be charged with harbouring, and thoroughly scared, he would be able to persuade her to apostatize. But so many possible agents were involved in the attacks upon recusants, that she might be arrested at some unexpected moment, without his knowledge. Would it not be more politic to be involved himself, to be ready, nay, eager, to see her house searched? (Her mother was no longer alive to reproach him.) Surely, enough evidence would be found to bring her into very serious trouble. Then he would have the glory of persuading her to conform. Her apostasy would be a great blow to the Catholic resistance movement . . . How pleased the Lord President would be!

The Earl of Huntingdon also knew when to attack and when to stay his hand. In September 1585 he started an intensive drive against recusants which filled the prisons. In the same month a young Catholic who had acted as school-master in the house of a gentleman named Marmaduke Bowes was arrested and, after torture, he apostatized. In despair, he betrayed several other people, including a priest, Fr Hugh Taylor, and Mr Bowes, whom he accused of har-bouring the priest since the passing of the statute.

In November, Fr Taylor and Mr Bowes were tried at the Castle, not by the Assize Judges but by the Council, whose plenary powers were greatly disliked by the common law-yers. On this occasion, Lord Evers (Vice-President) took the chair, with Laurence Meeres, Ralph Hurlestone and the secretary Henry Cheke forming the Bench. Fr Taylor was condemned, and executed two days later. Marmaduke Bowes, who until that time had been a 'church-Papist', conforming occasionally through fear of the laws, was indicted and condemned only upon the evidence of the apostate schoolmaster, whose unreliability was demon-strated in open court. Fr Taylor had in fact been arrested in another man's house, incidentally by Lord Evers himself. On 27 November, the day after Fr Taylor's execution, Mr Bowes, who had first been secretly reconciled to the Catholic Church, was hanged for harbouring him. This was the first execution in England for 'harbouring'.

Here was proof, indeed, that the provisions of the new Act were to be taken seriously, and that the Council intended to apply them by personal intervention if necessary. The death of Marmaduke Bowes created a great sensation in York, 'most men murmuring that this honest gentleman's life should be thus shamefully taken away'; they thought it 'loathsome and horrible'.

Margaret Clitherow was more circumspect in choosing a schoolmaster for her own children than Marmaduke Bowes had been. She obtained the services of the staunch Catholic, Brian Stapleton, who had spent nearly seven years in the Castle and had been her fellow-prisoner. His pupils, who included two or three other boys besides Margaret's own children, were given the run of the house in a way that Fr Mush thought imprudent, though, as he says, he did not know whether it was Margaret herself who showed the boys the secret entrance to the priest's room where the vestments and other Catholic articles were kept. She was often absent when something from the room was required, and 'the entry was painful to him that was not acquainted with the door, by reason of the straitness thereof, and yet large enough for a boy'.

On 15 January 1586, Henry May fulfilled his life's ambition, and 'by most voices of the Lord Mayor, Aldermen and Sheriffs' was elected Lord Mayor of York. On 3 February the seals of office were delivered to him. (On 15 February he married Anne Thomson at St Martin's church — an even grander wedding than Margaret's, for the Lord Mayor had two esquires and six sergeants-at-mace, all clothed in the city's livery. Probably he now began to repair his fortunes with the acquisition of the Drawswerde property in Davygate.)

The arraignment of the Lord Mayor's stepdaughter at the York Lent Assizes, 1586, on a capital charge, was the climax of the twelve-year battle between the ambitious man and the true and constant woman. Looking ahead to the record of his mayoralty, we can see that Henry May was intent on ingratiating himself with the Lord President of the Council.

The supreme moment of his life was to come in September 1586, after the thanksgiving festivities for the Queen's preservation from the Babington Conspiracy, when the renewal and extension of the Earl of Huntingdon's Commission as Lord-Lieutenant over the whole of the Council's area was celebrated. The Lord Mayor and Aldermen, in their red gowns, and many citizens in their best apparel, met the Earl 'at Walmgate Bar, the waits playing over the gates, and from thence brought him up into the city, with great store of torches and lights, Foss Bridge being very well perfumed with frankincense. And from thence the Lord Mayor and Sheriffs [and] their officers, did carry him to the Manor with torchlight.'

Three days later, summoned by the Lord President, the Lord Mayor, Aldermen and Twenty-Four went to the Common Hall, where the Lord President (Lord-Lieutenant) 'called the Lord Mayor to him, who came up to the bench on the right hand'; after the Commission of Lieutenancy had been read, 'the Lord Mayor did take the Sword from Mr Fawkes, sword-bearer, and *turning the point downward*, did deliver the same to the said Lord-Lieutenant, kissing the same with low reverence; and then the Lord-Lieutenant, holding the same in his hand a little while, did deliver it to the Lord Mayor again, *with the point downward*, who did deliver the same to Mr Fawkes, and then the Lord-Lieutenant made his exhortation; and the same ended, gave great thanks to the Lord Mayor, as well for his courteous entertainment, as also in that the said Lord Mayor, Aldermen and citizens had rejoiced . . . that Her Majesty had escaped the hands of her enemies.'[8]

In handing the sword to the Earl with the point downwards, Henry May was disobeying the Corporation's explicit instructions, that he should use such order in delivering up the sword as was used in 1581,[9] on a similar occasion when the Lieutenancy had first been granted; the sword had then been handed over with the point upwards.[10] The charter of King Richard II stated that the ceremonial Sword should be lowered only in the presence of the sovereign and his heirs; by this action Henry May created an embarrassing precedent and was possibly signalling to the Earl of Huntingdon a peculiar loyalty to his person. For Henry Hastings had a claim to the throne, by descent from George, Duke of Clarence; if not only the Catholic heiress, Mary, Queen of Scots, but her son also,[11] could be prevented from gaining the throne of England, the Puritan Earl of Huntingdon might become King Henry IX.

Henry May's action clearly reveals the nature of the man, ready to abase the city that had given him so much and fed his self-importance. (His name may be read to this day on the hilt of the Sword, refurbished for this very occasion.) In the face of such further possibilities for ambition, would he hesitate to use whatever means presented themselves, to tackle the problem of his recusant stepdaughter?

XII

Arrest

D URING the week before the Lent Assizes were due to
open, on Wednesday, 9 March 1586, the Council
ordered John Clitherow to appear before them. He
feared that he was to answer for his son's leaving the country,
and although he obeyed, he did not make his presence known
to them but hung about the Manor for a while, then 'departed,
seeing them so greatly busied in other matters'. On the 10th he
was called again; 'after some few words, they commanded him
to return to them again immediately after dinner, which he
did', reporting meanwhile the whole matter to his wife.

Margaret, so much more shrewd than her husband, 'feared
the worst' on hearing his news, and when he had gone 'she
came to the Father, which came to her but that morning, and
said: ". . . I pray God they intend no falsehood, and now,
whilst they have him, make my house to be searched. They pick
quarrels at me," quoth she, "and they will never cease until
they have me again, but God's will be done."' Clearly her
'discretion' had been such that her house had not been
searched before.

As Margaret suspected, 'so they deceitfully practised
indeed', continues Fr Mush, 'and sent forthwith the Sheriffs
of York' with several others, to search her house.

Now the Council in the North had their own pursuivant
and other officers, and normally preferred to trust their own
staff to make arrests, particularly in cases of recusancy. The
Corporation, by the Commission of 1578, had wide and
vague powers to search for priests, and where they had 'any

vehement presumption' of their presence, to 'cause the constables or some other public officer . . . to make search in the
house or houses that shall be so suspected. . . .'

The sheriffs, however, searched on warrants from the
Justices of the Peace, or else on orders from the High Commission. The chairman of the city Justices for this year was
Henry May, as Lord Mayor. Granted that for years all the
York authorities had co-operated in seeking out recusants,
the Lord President was careful to act legally, and his staff
would be expected to bear that in mind. They are unlikely to
have directly instigated the search of Margaret's house by
the sheriffs, but to have arranged for it together with the
Justices, or more probably, with Henry May alone.

The fact that John Clitherow put in an appearance at the
Manor, as ordered, on 9 March, and no search took place, is an
indication that too many people were involved for efficiency.
This abortive order might have been expected to act as an
advance warning, which could have defeated the object of the
search.

The most suspicious thing about the search is, however,
that it took place in the afternoon. In 1566 Pope Pius V had
forbidden any Mass to be said after midday (despite the
obvious benefits of flexibility), and this confirmation of the
medieval practice must have been very well known. No
priest would be found saying Mass in the afternoon, and
consequently no worshippers from outside would be present
in the house; evidence was sought, *but not too much*. It seems
there was no active desire to catch a priest, who would have
become the main focus of attention at the Assizes.

The intention evidently was to ensure that Margaret
Clitherow, who had previously appeared before the High
Commission and the Justices of the Peace in the company of
a small but determined band of obstinate recusants, should
now appear alone and unsupported before the full pomp of
the law, in the old-established form of the Westminster
judges on circuit. Once more her enemies intended, as Fr
Mush says, 'by terror and violence to weaken her strength, to
abate her courage, and to infringe her constancy'.

That the timing of Margaret's arrest had been deliberately engineered to suit her stepfather's interests may also be guessed from a civic custom introduced in 1580: it had then been agreed that 'the Judges and the Clerk of Assize shall yearly from henceforth dine at the Lord Mayor's place two times in the year, . . . on Monday in Lent Assize Week, and on Monday in Lammas Assize Week'. The purpose was immediately shown to be to give the Lord Mayor an opportunity to discuss with the judges various business relating to the city's concerns.[1]

The sheriffs for the year 1585–6 were Roland Fawcett, tailor, draper and innholder, and William Gibson, yeoman. After some argument, Fawcett had been appointed the senior, and he played the leading part in Margaret's arrest and in all that followed. He was no stranger to her and her family, for he too lived on the fringe of the Council in the North. (The son born to him in July 1586 had for one of his godparents Robert Man,[2] a wealthy clerk or attorney, formerly in the office of Thomas Eynns, Secretary to the Council until 1578. Robert Man had been a close friend of Margaret Clitherow's cousin Edward Turner,[3] the examining-clerk, in the same office.) He was a person upon whom the Council could rely.

The sheriffs, then, and their men, went to the house in the Shambles on the afternoon of Thursday, 10 March. They found Margaret 'occupied in her household business', not at formal prayer, though she 'feared the worst', but busied with the duties of her station. The entire routine of the house was proceeding as usual. 'The priest was in his chamber . . . in the next neighbour's house, and some other persons with him, and being forthwith certified of the searchers, they were all safely shifted away.'

'In a low chamber of her house'[4] — an attic — Mr Stapleton 'was quietly teaching his scholars, not knowing what was done in the house below', when 'a ruffian bearing a sword and buckler on his arm, opened the chamber door, and suspecting the schoolmaster to be a priest, he shut again the door, and called his fellows. The schoolmaster, thinking him to be a friend, opened the door to call him in; but when he perceived the matter, he shut the door again, and by that way, which was from the martyr's house to the priest's chamber, escaped their paws. The searchers, greedy of a prey, came in great haste to the chamber, and not finding him, they raged like madmen, and as though he had been a priest indeed, took all the children, the servants, and the martyr away with them. At this time they searched chests, coffers, and every corner of her house; but, as I learned,' says Fr Mush, 'they found nothing of any importance.'

They therefore turned their attention to the children in their custody. There was one whom Fr Mush usually calls 'the Flemish boy' because he 'was born in Flanders of an Englishman and a Dutch woman, and had been brought from thence almost two years before'; he was about ten or twelve years old. This boy they stripped, 'and with rods threatened him, standing naked amongst them, unless he would tell them all they asked. The child, fearing that cruelty, yielded, and brought them to the priest his chamber, wherein was a conveyance [i.e. secret contrivance] for books and church stuff, which he revealed.' There were signs of recent occupation in the room as two or three apple tarts and some bread had been left behind. 'They took the spoil', and moreover, adding private theft to the performance of their duties, they 'conveyed two or three beds away as their own.'

'The children and the servants were all sent to divers prisons', and so for Anne Clitherow and for Margaret's other children — the youngest was probably five years old — their years of personal suffering for the Faith began, at a very tender age.

The sheriffs' most important prisoner, Margaret Clitherow, was taken immediately to the Manor and brought before the Council, or rather, before such members as were in attendance, the same four men who had condemned Marmaduke Bowes: the Vice-President, Lord Evers, Laurence Meeres, Ralph Hurlestone and Henry Cheke. 'Being merry and stout for the Catholic cause' Margaret 'thereby moved their fury vehemently against her, especially by her smiling cheerful countenance, and the small esteem she made of their cruel threats and railing.'

John Clitherow was also at the Manor, and both were kept there separately until night, 'when about seven of the clock they committed the martyr unto close prison to the Castle'. Margaret arrived there soaked to the skin, having to rely on the charity of the other prisoners to lend her 'all kinds of apparel' while her own dried out. (In 1581 a ducking stool had been set in St George's Close,[5] by the river and near the Castle; the nearest way from the Manor to the Castle was by the river; had Margaret become the sport of the sheriffs' sergeants and been ducked as a scold? She offered no explanation of her condition; Fr Mush's informants said there had been no rain.) An hour later John Clitherow was sent to a separate room in the Castle.

The following day, a General Sessions of the Peace was held for the city, before the Lord Mayor and two aldermen; the sheriffs attended as usual. It fell to the sheriffs to pick the juries for all trials in the city, as Margaret would have known; on this occasion, the juries included, among other familiar names, Christopher Smithson, draper (to whose son John Clitherow in 1582 had stood godfather), and one of far greater, and more poignant, significance: William Tesimond.[6]

Tesimond's spirit had finally been broken in 1583: he had conformed and gone to church.[7] His devotion to Thomas Percy, his outspoken confession of faith before the High Commission, his constancy in the frozen stocks, none of these things had availed him in the end.

It was the practice of the sheriffs to pick juries from the same limited section of the community, so that the same individuals frequently served; if the news reaching Margaret's ears included the appearance of the lamented William Tesimond as a juryman on this day, she may well have started thinking about his dilemma, if he were to be picked the following week for the Assizes also. How many members of the grand and petty juries might be persons whose hearts were still Catholic, as his was?[8]

Meanwhile the wretched Flemish boy had given the Council a list of names, duly recorded by the secretary, of people he had seen at Mass at Margaret's house; one of these was her old friend Mrs Anne Tesh, who joined her in her room at the Castle on the following Saturday. Mrs Tesh found Margaret 'so merry and joyful of her trouble, that she would say, she feared to offend God thereby'. At the same time she 'kept great abstinence and prayer'.

When the rumours flying around the city became sufficiently alarming a messenger was found to bring them to Margaret, no doubt as part of the war of nerves, and in the hope of incriminating her and others. The story went that the Flemish boy 'had accused her for harbouring and maintaining divers priests, but especially two by name, that was, Mr Francis Ingleby of Rheims, and Mr John Mush of Rome. It was reported withal that she should suffer for it according to the new law and statute,' that is, that she would be hanged.

The effect of this news upon Margaret was not at all what the messenger expected. She laughed and said, 'I would I had some good thing to give you for these good news. Hold, take this fig, for I have nothing better.'

Once during these few days Margaret 'was permitted to speak with her husband in the audience of the gaoler and other more, but she never saw him after', although the friends of both tried hard to obtain permission for another meeting between them. The price demanded for it was an act of apostasy. Friendship now was of no avail.

On Monday, 14 March, the first day of the Assizes, Margaret expected to be called to the court, when she would hear her indictment read, and would learn officially with what crime she had been charged.

Margaret 'made herself ready', donning the high-crowned hat which merchants' wives commonly wore; but the whole morning passed and she was not called. She and Anne Tesh laughed and talked together as they waited, and sometimes Margaret said, 'Sister, we are so merry together that I fear unless we be parted we shall hazard to lose the merit of our imprisonment.'

'A little before she was called to the judges, she said, "Yet, before I go, I will make all my brethren and sisters on the other side the hall merry."' These 'brethren and sisters' were of course the fellow-Catholics to whom she often referred in this way. 'Looking forth of a window towards them—they were five-and-thirty, and might easily behold her from thence—she made a pair of gallows on her fingers, and pleasantly [i.e. jokingly] laughed at them.'

Margaret had often longed to give spiritual comfort to Catholics in prison, 'to ease the griefs of such as were there discontented', for she could 'not abide to hear that in their distresses any should murmur'. Now she was trying to encourage them, since they had heard of her danger. She was attempting to teach them, quite literally, to 'be *glad* of every cross for Christ's sake'.

At last, 'after dinner', about one o'clock, 'the gaoler told her how she must go even then before the judges. "Well," quoth she, "God be thanked, I am ready when you please."'

XIII

Arraignment

MARGARET CLITHEROW had prepared for this summons with great abstinence and prayer. However little attention she had seemed to give to the report that she was to be condemned under the statute against harbouring priests, the sign she made to the other Catholic prisoners showed that she expected to suffer the penalty laid down by this statute.

How far had she considered what would happen in the court room? She was utterly convinced that whatever the procedure it would result in her death. She said later to a friend, 'The Council . . . earnestly seek my blood . . . it must needs be done.' For ten years she had been known to the Council, ten years during which the laws against recusancy had been gradually tightened up and applied more stringently. She must, on previous appearances in court, before the Justices of the Peace and the High Commission, have heard much abuse and many threats, often from the same people sitting as judges in different capacities. Now, on entering the Common Hall (the Guildhall) where the Assizes were being held,[1] she saw upon the Bench a most imposing array of figures: Lord Evers, Vice-President[2] of the Council in the North, sat between Judges Clench[3] (who had condemned to death Fathers Lacey and Kirkman, and probably Fr Hart also) and Rodes[4] (long familiar in York as a legal member of the Council), the two common law judges on circuit (wearing scarlet robes); the two legal Councillors currently in residence, Laurence Meeres and Ralph

Hurlestone (who had already questioned Margaret at the Manor) were in places of honour, and the Secretary, Henry Cheke (son of Fr Henry Comberford's former colleague, Edward VI's tutor) was also present.[5] Even more alarming, perhaps, was it to see her stepfather, the Lord Mayor, and the entire bench of aldermen,[6] all wearing for this first day of the Assizes, their scarlet gowns. The two sheriffs also wore scarlet — wherever she looked she saw the colour of blood — and all the liveried servants were there, the swordbearer, the macebearer, the Lord Mayor's six sergeants-at-mace and the sheriffs' four sergeants.

This was the first time that Margaret had appeared in court before her stepfather; he seems to have deliberately avoided such an encounter. It was also her first appearance at the Assizes, and from the fact that she was called immediately after dinner, we may deduce that her indictment appeared first on the file. (Felonies were taken before misdemeanours.[7])

Margaret was later to declare herself 'not skilful in the temporal laws'. She had discussed with Fr Mush the dangers of her situation, but he had actually told her to 'prepare her neck for the rope'; this and the Councillors' 'cruel threats' must have contributed very considerably to her conviction that the Council intended her death. She had accepted the threats quite simply as future punishments inescapable except by an action the very thought of which she would not entertain for an instant, namely, apostasy.

For apostasy was the real aim of all the measures against recusants; that was proved in countless instances on the scaffold. But to loyal Catholics the alternative to recusancy was something worse than the death of the body, for what shall a man give in exchange for his soul?

Margaret stood at the bar, 'not having any counsel . . . desolate of all human comfort'. Persons on trial in the sixteenth century on criminal charges had to conduct their own defence. She could only be guided by her own discretion, enlightened by prayer and by the words of Jesus Christ to his disciples: 'Beware of men. For they will deliver you up in councils . . . and you shall be brought before governors and before kings for my sake. . . . But when they shall deliver you up, take no thought how or what to speak: for it shall be given you in that hour what to speak. For it is not you that speak, but the Spirit of your Father that speaketh in you' (Matt. 10. 16–20). 'For the Holy Ghost shall teach you in the same hour what you must say' (Luke 12. 12).

Margaret stood, then, at the bar and heard her indictment read. The words of a criminal indictment were as horrible as the punishments. Margaret's indictment has not survived, all the Assize records for the Northern circuit of earlier date than 1607 having been lost through the ravages of time, but while these records were still in existence, Richard Smith, Bishop of Chalcedon (the second bishop sent at last to England, Wales and Scotland, in 1624) had them searched for the purposes of checking and adding to the official lists of martyrs. The precise crime with which Margaret was charged was found in the Assize register: it was the harbouring of Francis Ingleby.[8]

Though the general gist of an indictment was the same, details of the basic wording varied slightly from writer to writer; but the crime was always an offence against God as well as man. Margaret's indictment can be reconstructed from that included in the official account of the trials of Robert Barnes and Jane Wiseman, charged in Middlesex in 1598 with harbouring George Hathersall.[9] In the tense atmosphere of the court, Margaret heard the following accusation read:

'Whereas Francis Ingleby late of Ripley in the county of Yorkshire, clerk, born within the dominions of our lady Elizabeth by the grace of god of England France and Ireland Queen, Defender of the Faith etc., was, after the Feast of the Nativity of St John the Baptist which was in the first year of the reign of the said lady now Queen, and before the first day of March in the eight and twentieth year of the reign of the said lady now Queen, by authority derived from the See of Rome, at Laon in France in parts

beyond the seas, made and ordained priest, a certain
Margaret Clitherow late of the parish of Holy Trinity
King's Court in the city of York, wife of John Clitherow
citizen and butcher of York, not having the fear of God
before her eyes but moved and seduced by the instigation
of the Devil, knowing the same Francis Ingleby to be a
priest by stealth, on the tenth day of March[10] in the eight
and twentieth year aforesaid, the same Francis Ingleby in
the city of York aforesaid did wittingly, willingly and
feloniously receive, comfort, aid and maintain, against the
form of the statute in that case set forth and provided, and
against the peace of the said lady now Queen, her crown
and dignities etc.' (the statute being the Act 'against
Jesuits, seminary priests and other such like disobedient
persons').

There was a brief pause after the reading of the indictment,
while all the onlookers regarded her, and Judge Clench
looked with curiosity and pity—for he was a mild-natured
man and no bigot—at the 'comely, beautiful young
woman', 'about thirty years of age', who stood at the bar,
composed and smiling, unwittingly defying the conventions
by appearing in court still wearing her hat.[11] So this was the
Lord Mayor's stepdaughter; he had just been hearing something of her history, while at dinner with the Lord Mayor.
Clench stood up and opened the proceedings:

CLENCH: Margaret Clitherow, how say you? Are you
guilty of this indictment, or no?

At this point she was told to remove the offending hat.

MARGARET ('*mildly, with a bold* [*i.e. fearless*] *and smiling
countenance*'): I know no offence whereof I should confess
myself guilty.

CLENCH: Yes, you have harboured and maintained
Jesuits and priests, enemies to her Majesty.

124

This apparent acceptance of the wording of the indictment as proof of guilt was customary in criminal proceedings.

MARGARET: I never knew nor have harboured any such persons, or maintained those which are not the Queen's friends. God defend [i.e. forbid] I should.

Margaret had not replied to the first question in the form of words expected, either 'Guilty' or 'Not guilty'. If the account is accurate, the fact that the arraignment was not held up at this point must mean that the judge, lenient towards what he supposed was a woman's ignorance, instructed the clerk of the court to record a plea of Not guilty.

CLENCH: How will you be tried?

The correct, formal answer to this was 'by God and the country [i.e. jury]'; it implied neither guilt nor innocence. Instead of making this formal reply which would allow the proceedings to continue, Margaret made a simple statement which went to the heart of the matter, and challenged the right of the state to make laws against the Catholic religion.

MARGARET: Having made no offence, I need no trial.

She seemed to be feeling her way step by step, taking her cue from what was said to her.

CLENCH & RODES: You have offended the statutes, and therefore you must be tried. How will you be tried?
MARGARET: If you say I have offended, and that I must be tried, I will be tried by none but by God and your own consciences.
CLENCH: No, you cannot so do, for we sit here to see justice and law, and therefore you must be tried by the country.

MARGARET: I will be tried by none but by God and your
own consciences.

Here, a sacrilegious and farcical interlude was allowed to
take place, which must have greatly enhanced the already
dramatic nature of the scene. (Fr Mush called the whole
arraignment a 'pageant'.)

'Then they brought forth two chalices, divers pictures,
and in mockery put two vestments and other church gear
upon two lewd fellows' backs, and in derision the one began
to pull and dally with the other, scoffing before the judges on
the bench, and holding up singing breads [i.e. unconse-
crated hosts], said to the martyr: "Behold thy gods in whom
thou believest."'

CLENCH & RODES: How do you like those vestments?
MARGARET: I like them well, if they were on their backs
that know to use them to God's honour, as they were
made.
CLENCH (*standing up*): In whom believe you?
MARGARET: I believe in God.
CLENCH: In what God?
MARGARET: I believe in God the Father, in God the Son,
and God the Holy Ghost; in these Three Persons and
One God I fully believe, and that by the passion, death,
and merits of Christ Jesu I must be saved.
CLENCH: You say well.

There was a pause here, while the Bench took counsel
among themselves. They were no further forward; unless the
defendant gave the formal answer and agreed to be tried 'by
God and the country' the case could not be heard. The law
provided a terrible means of forcing defendants to plead.
After a while the judges returned to the attack.

CLENCH & RODES: Margaret Clitherow, how say you
yet? Are you content to be tried by God and the
country?

126

MARGARET: No.

CLENCH: Good woman, consider well what you do; if you refuse to be tried by the country, you make yourself guilty and accessory to your own death, for we cannot try you but by order of law. You need not fear this kind of trial, for I think the country cannot find you guilty upon this slender evidence of a child.[12]

But still Margaret refused to be tried. They changed the subject again.

CLENCH & RODES: Was not your husband privy to your doings in keeping priests?

This was a trick question; whether she answered 'Yes' or 'No', would be an admission to keeping priests, though in itself it would not bring her trial any nearer. Her answer showed she had realized the trap and avoided it; at the same time it completely cleared John Clitherow of complicity. Nobody who heard the tone of her voice would think she was shielding him.

MARGARET: God knoweth I could never yet get my husband in that good case that he were worthy to know or come in place where they were to serve God.

CLENCH: We must proceed by law against you, which will condemn you to a sharp death for want of trial.

MARGARET *('cheerfully')*: God's will be done: I thank God I may suffer any death for this good cause.

She did not wonder what this 'sharp death' would be; she took what came. That it would be death that came she had never doubted.

'Some of them said, seeing her joy, that she was mad, and possessed with a smiling spirit.' Judge Rodes 'also railed against her on the Catholic faith and priests; so did also the other Councillors, and Mr Hurlestone openly before them all said: "It is not for religion that thou harbourest priests,

127

but for whoredom;" and furiously uttered such like slanders, sitting on the Bench.

'The Bench rose that night without pronouncing any sentence against her, and she was brought from the Hall with a great troop of men and halberds, with a smiling and most cheerful countenance, dealing money on both sides the streets, to John Trewe's house on the bridge, where she was shut up in a close parlour.'

Her route lay along Coney Street, past St Martin's church, so full of associations for Margaret, along Spurriergate, and down Ousegate to the bridge.

'John Trewe's house ', or the New Counter, was a superior prison built by the Corporation some thirteen years before, and fitted up by certain prisoners at their own expense. It was situated on the north side of Ouse Bridge, between the two Kidcote prisons and the old chapel dedicated to St William of York, which now formed part of a group of official buildings. The upper portion of the chapel, converted into a dwelling house by the addition of flooring, made a continuation of the prison. The New Counter had, on the side facing the river, two mullioned windows, surmounted by gables.

In this prison Margaret's friend Mrs Vavasour had already spent more than four years. Fr Mush does not dare to mention her by name as she was still there when he wrote, but undoubtedly she was one of the 'honest and credible' witnesses on whom he had to rely for all his information about Margaret's last days.

On this Monday evening Margaret took stock of her position, 'praying upon her knees', examining her conscience at length, as was her daily custom. What she had so far done was in effect to deny that Caesar had any competence over the things of God. An anonymous writer, almost certainly Fr Mush himself, says of her, 'This happy martyr knowing her cause to be so just and godly, that neither any human law could justly reprove it, nor any profane [i.e. temporal] judge be competent by any pretence of equity to deal against her for her religious works and Christian duty . . . refused common trial of the country. . . . '[13]

She was in effect making the same point as St Thomas More, after his own condemnation fifty years earlier: 'This indictment is grounded upon an Act of Parliament directly repugnant to the laws of God and his Holy Church . . .; it is therefore in law, amongst Christian men, insufficient to charge any Christian man'.[14]

Now Margaret may have considered more fully what the position of the jurors would be if her case went forward for trial, and she realized that she had been providentially led into a course of action that would spare them all. She explained this later to a friend, perhaps Mrs Vavasour: 'If I should have put myself to the country, evidence must needs have come against me which I know none could give but only my children and servants. And it would have been more grievous to me than a thousand deaths if I should have seen any of them brought forth before me to give evidence against me. Secondly, I knew well the country must needs have found me guilty to please the Council, which earnestly seek my blood; and then all they had been accessory to my death, and damnably offended God. I thought it therefore in the way of charity on my part to hinder the country from such a sin; and since it must needs be done, to cause as few to do it as might be; and that was the judge himself.'

In fact, such was the situation of the defendant on a criminal charge, that Margaret had been unaware until the judge referred to 'this slender evidence of a child', that the only witness was still the Flemish boy. (That in itself was suspicious in the circumstances. She might have expected some of the other children — and her servants were probably children too — to break down under interrogation, for they had all been sent to prison.) On analysis, the first part of her explanation to her friend can only apply to her state of mind before her arraignment opened; she had therefore entered the court already determined not to plead.

From this point onwards, the situation of the jury, *sworn* to try the issue without fear or favour, must have engrossed her thoughts. The Protestant sheriff who had already empanelled William Tesimond for the Quarter Sessions was

129

quite likely to choose him again, or others in a similar situation, in an attempt to force them into a deeper kind of conformity. Moreover, both her neighbour William Calvert and her own brother George Middleton were liable to jury service.[15]

The old English criminal law was notoriously devoid of justice. A modern scholar states that in the sixteenth century the impartiality of both sheriff and juror could rarely be guaranteed, and that by the fifteen-seventies, the right of the the judges to threaten juries, either before or after their verdict, in order to secure a decision in accordance with the wishes of the bench, was an accepted convention.[16] Not until 1670 would the right of a jury to return an independent verdict be established. The historian Henry Hallam (son of a canon of Windsor) condemns the 'glaring transgressions of natural as well as positive law that rendered our courts of justice in cases of treason' — and in related cases — 'little better than *the caverns of murderers*'. (John Mush himself could not have expressed it more strongly.) He particularly mentions the contribution made by 'a passive pusillanimous jury'.[17]

Fifty years before Margaret Clitherow's arraignment, one of the grand juries chosen by the Duke of Norfolk for the arraignment in York of the leaders of the Pilgrimage of Grace had included many kinsmen of the defendants, since this, as he told Thomas Cromwell, would 'prove their affections. . . . And if they will not find [a true bill], then they may have thanks according to their cankered hearts' (that is, enormous fines and indefinite imprisonment).

Margaret Clitherow's jury was likely to contain two classes of men: those who could be relied upon to find her guilty, and those who would not dare to find her innocent. If the jury is seen, not as an impersonal mass, but as a number of individuals chosen to play a certain part, Margaret's action in continuing her refusal to be tried becomes fully intelligible as an act of supreme charity.

There was, however, yet another reason for her refusal, one that Fr Mush, writing so soon after the event, did not dare to mention. When Margaret 'hired' a room in her neighbour's house, she had probably seen that it was completely sealed off from the other house, in the manner of many internal rearrangements made in the sixteenth and seventeenth centuries. Nevertheless, it was under her neighbour's roof, and that neighbour, whether Millicent Calvert, John Clitherow's sister, or his kinsfolk, Michael and Ellen Mudd, must have been in a state of great apprehension.

Margaret's silence protected equally the weaker Catholics who were her next-door neighbours, and those with whom the juries might have been half-packed. She was already well-practised in keeping silence when reproached and contradicted, returning 'to the comfort of her inward mind and conscience'.

A Latin work on the recent martyrs, published at Antwerp in 1592, but licensed in 1587, makes no mention of the jurymen's consciences or of Margaret's fear of betrayal by her children; it says, 'She was condemned to an extremely cruel death because she refused to answer as they wished or to name anyone else, and was unwilling to be the cause of another's death or to bring him to the misfortune of such terrible sufferings and to give him occasion for the shipwreck of his faith.'[18]

Margaret's prayers were interrupted this evening by one visitor, the well-known Puritan preacher Giles Wigginton, vicar of Sedbergh in the West Riding. He was a scholar, in many ways a very simple, even a foolish man; he was also clearly of a kind and even-tempered disposition, and he was to prove himself both charitable and courageous. Now he came to the prison and 'ministered talk' to Margaret 'as their fashion is', says Fr Mush contemptuously; but he was a mere distraction to her at this most important moment of her life. She 'regarded him very little, and desired him not to trouble her', in fact she sent him about his business rather sharply, ' "for your fruits", quoth she, "are correspondent to your doctrine" '. Nevertheless, he did not take offence, but departed.

'All that night she remained in that parlour', together with a couple named Yoward, who had been imprisoned for debt. There was a special prison for debtors on the other side of the bridge, and from the fact that Fr Mush, in his usual excessive manner, calls this couple 'two evil-disposed persons of their own sect', that is, Protestant, it is likely that they had been chosen for transfer to the New Counter in the hope of influencing Margaret. Nothing else is recorded by Fr Mush of Yoward, but his wife appears as a good-hearted soul who quite forgot her own distress in the presence of Margaret's infinitely greater trouble, and who did her best to comfort her in her own way.

The following morning, about eight o'clock, Margaret was brought once more to the Common Hall to stand at the bar. The proceedings were then reopened.

CLENCH: Margaret Clitherow, how say you yet? Yester-night we passed you over without judgement, which we might have then pronounced against you if we would: we did it not, hoping you would be something more conformable, and put yourself to the country, for otherwise you must needs have the law. We see nothing why you should refuse; here be but small witness against you, and the country will consider your case.

MARGARET: Indeed, I think you have no witnesses against me but children, which with an apple and a rod you may make to say what you will.

CLENCH & RODES: It is plain that you had priests in your house by these things which were found.

MARGARET: As for good Catholic priests, I know no cause why I should refuse them as long as I live; they come only to do me good and others.

Here the Councillor Hurlestone interrupted, joining with Judge Rodes and others in outraged exclamation.

RODES, HURLESTONE & OTHERS: They are all traitors, rascals, and deceivers of the Queen's subjects.

MARGARET: God forgive you. You would not say so of them if you knew them.

RODES & OTHERS: You would detest them yourself if you knew their treason and wickedness as we do.

MARGARET: I know them for virtuous men, sent by God only to save our souls.

'These speeches and the like she uttered very boldly [i.e. confidently] and with great modesty.'

CLENCH: What say you? Will you put yourself to the country, yea or no?

MARGARET: I see no cause why I should do so in this matter: I refer my cause only to God and your own consciences. Do what you think good.

'All the people about her condemned her of great obstinacy and folly, that she would not yield; and on every hand persuaded [i.e. urged] her to refer her trial to the country, which could not find her guilty, as they said, upon such slender evidence; but she would not.'

CLENCH: Well, we must pronounce a sentence against you. Mercy lieth in our hands, in the country's also, if you put your trial to them; otherwise you must have the law.

At this point the Puritan preacher Giles Wigginton interrupted the proceedings. He was exercising the right of intervening as *amicus curiae* (friend of the court), to inform the judge of an error he had noticed. It is interesting to observe, in view of this man's subsequent history of ineptitude — he became to some extent involved with the lunatic Hacket — that he had completely misunderstood the legal points involved. He clearly thought that the judge was about to pass sentence as though the boy's evidence had been heard; he did not realize that there had been no trial and could be no trial unless or until Margaret gave way, and that the sanction about to be pronounced, provisionally, was the normal procedure in cases where the defendant stood 'mute of malice'.

He 'stood up and called to the Judge on the Bench, saying, "My lord, give me leave to speak;" but the murmuring and noise in the Hall would not suffer him to be heard: yet he continued still calling that he might speak, and the Judge commanded silence to hear him.'

> WIGGINTON: My lord, take heed what you do. You sit here to do justice; this woman's case is touching life and death — you ought not, either by God's laws or man's, to judge her to die upon the slender witness of a boy; nor unless you have two or three sufficient men of very good credit to give evidence against her. Therefore, look to it, my lord, this gear goeth sore [i.e. this is a serious matter].
> CLENCH: I may do it by law.
> WIGGINTON: By what law?
> CLENCH: By the Queen's law.
> WIGGINTON: That may well be, but you cannot do it by God's law.

'And he said no more.'
The Judge addressed Margaret again.

> CLENCH: Good woman, I pray you put yourself to the country. There is no evidence but a boy against you, and whatsoever they do, yet we may show mercy afterward.

But Margaret still refused to plead.

It was a deadlock. The Judge paused, reluctant to utter the dreadful penalty. He sat there irresolute, as though he, and not the composed young woman before him, were the defendant, and she the judge. Then Judge Rodes lost all patience. He burst out:

134

RODES: Why stand we all this day about this naughty, wilful woman? Let us dispatch her.[19]

Judge Clench realized that he was bound to break the deadlock by decreeing the terrible punishment of *peine forte et dure*, but he still made it conditional, leaving the door open for a change of attitude in Margaret.

CLENCH: If you will not put yourself to the country this must be your judgement. You must return from whence you came, and there, in the lowest part of the prison, be stripped naked, laid down, your back upon the ground, and as much weight laid upon you as you are able to bear, and so to continue three days without meat or drink, except a little barley bread and puddle water, and the third day to be pressed to death, your hands and feet tied to posts, and a sharp stone under your back.

Margaret later described what her reaction had been when she heard the sentence: 'Neither did I fear the terror of the sentence of death, but was ashamed on their behalfs to have such shameful words uttered in that audience as to strip me naked, and press me to death among men, which methought for womanhood they might have concealed.' She was indeed 'unskilled in the temporal laws' to imagine that the judge was free to conceal part of the traditional wording of the penalty! It is clear, too, that until that moment she had not known what the penalty would be.

She was able to disguise her feeling of shame, and answered 'without any fear or change of countenance'.

MARGARET: If this judgement be according to your own conscience, I pray God send you better judgement before him. I thank God heartily for this.

Clench reacted with considerable warmth. His office had forced him to utter these words against his will. He strongly

denied Margaret's suggestion that it was his personal judgement, and added a further plea to her. (In fact, whereas the
law required a triple warning of this sanction, Clench
warned and pleaded with Margaret Clitherow no less than
seven times, and gave judgement provisionally; this was a
personal act of mercy, for which the statutes and text-books
made no allowance.) He was deeply touched by the situation
in which Margaret had placed herself. A family man himself — he had fifteen children — he appealed to her natural
affections.

> CLENCH: Nay, I do it according to law, and tell you this
> must be your judgement, unless you put yourself to be
> tried by the country. Consider of it, you have husband
> and children to care for; cast not yourself away.

Margaret answered in supernatural terms reminiscent of
the first ages of the Church and the earliest era of
persecution.

> MARGARET: I would to God my husband and children
> might suffer with me for so good a cause.

This was too much for the sixteenth century to stomach.
'Upon which words the heretics reported after, that she
would both have hanged her husband and children if she
could.'
The Judge made one last plea to her to change her mind,
in which case he would gladly withdraw the sentence.

> CLENCH: How say you, Margaret Clitherow? Are you
> content to put yourself to the trial of the country?
> Although we have given sentence [20] against you accord-
> ing to the law, yet will we show mercy, if you will do
> anything yourself.
> MARGARET (*'lifting up her eyes towards heaven, . . . with a
> cheerful countenance'*): God be thanked, all that he shall
> send me shall be welcome; I am not worthy of so good a

death as this is ; I have deserved death for mine offences
to God, but not for anything that I am accused of.

'*I am not worthy of so good a death as this is.*' Many of the
martyrs used such words, but there may be a further meaning here. Margaret had heard the sentence for the first time;
had it already occurred to her that when she was laid on her
back and her hands and feet were tied to posts she would
probably die in the same attitude as her Master?

'Then the Judge bade the sheriff look to her, who pinioned
her arms with a cord. The martyr first beholding the one arm
and then the other, smiled to herself and was joyful to be
bound with Christ for Christ's sake; at which they all raged
against her. So the sheriff brought her with halberds to the
bridge again, where she was before. Some of the Bench sent
to mark her countenance as she was carried forth of the Hall,
but she departed from thence through the streets with joyful
countenance, whereat some said, "It must needs be that she
received comfort from the Holy Ghost", for all were
astonished to see her of so good cheer. Some said it was not
so, but that she was possessed with a merry devil, and that
she sought her own death.

'The two sheriffs brought her between them, she dealing
money on both sides as she could, being pinioned.

'After this none was permitted to speak with her but
ministers, and such as were appointed by the Council.'

XIV

The Last Battles

WHEN the outcome of Margaret's arraignment was
made known, the city was in an uproar. The stepdaughter of the Lord Mayor — 'daughter', they
would call her — the wife of a prominent citizen known to
everyone, condemned to death, and by so barbarous and
medieval a means! It was a first-class sensation. And everyone wanted to know how it had come about, why she had
been so adamant in her refusal to stand trial, and, above all,
whether the punishment would actually be carried out.
Which would give way, Margaret Clitherow or the Council?
And soon they realized that there was one way out that
would save the faces of both. A pregnant woman was never
executed until after the birth of her child. Some friend of
Margaret's remembered that she had dropped a hint that
she might be pregnant. This was enough to start a fresh
rumour about her, which soon reached the ears of the Judges
themselves.

On the day after Margaret's condemnation, Fawcett, the
senior sheriff, who would be mainly responsible for carrying
out the penalty, 'came to Clench, and demanded what he
should do with her. The Judge answered, "She may not be
executed, for they say she is with child."

'Rodes, Meeres, Hurlestone, Cheke, and the rest urged
sore that she might be executed according to judgement and
law.[1] And Mr Rodes said, "Brother Clench, you are, too
merciful in these cases; if she had not law she would undo a
great many."'

Then Judge Clench put his foot down and exerted his own authority, clearly hating his task.

' "If she be with child," he said, "I will not consent that she shall die."

' "Then," quoth the sheriff, "my lord, I shall make a quest of women to go upon her." '

Clench was sickened by this proposal: a legal 'inquest' or 'jury of matrons' would involve questioning and examination by twelve women accustomed to dealing in this way with the criminal class. Had not Mistress Clitherow suffered enough indignity at the hands of the law? — and God alone knew what still lay before her. At that moment Judge Clench must have felt great revulsion for his profession.

'It needeth not,' he said shortly. 'Call four honest women, which know her well, and let them try it.'

At least strangers would not be involved; he spared her that.

The next day the four women joined the stream of callers permitted by the Council to visit Margaret. They 'returned answer to the Judge, that she was with child as far as they could perceive or gather by her own words'. In their anxiety both to gain a reprieve for her and to tell the Judge what he wished to hear, they stated the case more strongly than Margaret did, for the same day she was asked the same question, Was she with child? by no less an assembly of persons than Sir Thomas Fairfax, a Vice-President of the Council, Lawrence Meeres, and other Councillors.

Her reply was cool, impersonal, precise; one could never guess that her very life depended upon it, as she weighed the evidence: 'She said she knew not certainly, and would not for all the world take it on her conscience either that she was with child or that she was not, but if she were it was very young, and as she thought rather she was than otherwise. . . . After this they went to the Judge, and told him what she had said.'

'That night, or the next day, Hurlestone,[2] the Councillors, and ministers . . . came to Clench in his chamber and said, "My lord, this woman is not to have the benefit of her belly, for that she hath refused trial by the country, and the sentence of death is passed against her." '

Clench, a good common law judge — the Queen used to call him 'my good judge' — answered heatedly, 'Mr Hurlestone, God defend she should die, if she be with child; although she hath offended, yet hath not the child in her womb. I will not for a thousand pounds, therefore, give my consent until she be further tried.' He wished her to be given the 'benefit of the *venter*', which enabled any woman at all likely to be pregnant to have her execution deferred for twenty weeks at least.

'Hurlestone urged still and said, "*She is the only woman in the north parts*, and if she be suffered to live, there will be more of her order without any fear of law. And therefore, my lord, consider with yourself," quoth he, "and let her have law according to judgement passed, for I will take it upon my conscience that she is not with child."

'The Judge would by no means consent; but, thinking to wash his hands with Pilate, referred all to the Council,[3] and willed them to do their own discretions; and at his departure he commanded to stay the execution till Friday after . . . and then to do as they should think good, if in the meantime they heard not from him to the contrary.'

So Judge Clench passes out of the story. He was a kind man, and the situation grieved him, not merely because he was a common lawyer who was uneasy with the statute laws and with the conciliar form of government with which he had to work in the North. He had been deeply affected by Margaret's case and it is unlikely that he ever forgot that beautiful young woman with her unshakeable poise and serene determination, nor the unearthly look upon her face after he had pronounced the penalty against her.

Margaret's kinsfolk and friends continued their efforts to force her to say definitely that she was pregnant, 'but she would never affirm it of any certainty, but said she would not dissemble with God and the world,' for she had 'been deceived heretofore in this'. They must have brought her news, too, of her husband and children, hoping to break down her constancy by the consideration of their grief and sufferings. 'When her husband heard that they had condemned her, he fared like a man out of his wits, and wept so vehemently that the blood gushed out of his nose in great quantity, and said, "Alas! will they kill my wife? Let them take all I have and save her, for she is the best wife in all England, and the best Catholic also." ' Her eldest daughter, Anne, who was about twelve years old, 'was at the first committed to ward [i.e. prison] because she would not betray her mother, and there extremely used for that she would not go to the church'.

During these days when it still seemed possible that the execution of the penalty would be further postponed or even forbidden, Margaret managed to send word by a trusted friend to Fr Mush in hiding, 'desiring him to pray earnestly for her, for it was the heaviest cross that ever came to her, that she feared she should escape death'. To be reprieved but strictly imprisoned would be a far worse punishment, robbing her not only of the martyr's crown in eternity but also of the sacraments in life, a deprivation which she had always 'accounted death'. She felt 'still that she was not worthy to suffer such a death for God his sake', but set herself to prepare for it 'with much prayer and fasting'.[4] In fact, 'from her first coming to the bridge . . . her diet was a water pottage, rye bread, and small ale, which she took but once a day, and that in little quantity'.

All the time she was afraid, not of death, but of her own weakness. She feared that she might try to rely on herself; 'flesh is frail', she continually reminded herself. She had long had 'a reverent and a necessary fear of her own weakness, that might easily slide to . . . follies, unless it were daily strengthened with God's grace'. She had moreover seen many convinced Catholics fall 'from the unity of Christ's Church', even some who had endured intense suffering for the Faith; were not these people, and the mortal danger to their souls, constantly in her mind and her prayers?

She who understood other people so well, knew the hidden motives she herself might have for her actions. For years she had suspected 'her own actions . . . to be impure in the sight of God', and she had desired the company of those who judged hardly of her, so that she might see for herself and amend her hidden imperfections. She felt 'she might offend God in every of her actions', and for this reason had given up her own will to be guided by her confessor, as the only safe course. It was, too, the vow of obedience that made religious life especially attractive to her.

Now, only the will of God must be considered; if she obtruded her own will to ask for postponement of the execution she might fail altogether. She saw clearly that she could easily deceive herself and believe that it was consideration for an unborn child — whose very existence was uncertain — that motivated an appeal for clemency. During those twenty weeks' reprieve that the 'benefit of the *venter*' would give her, might not consideration for her other children overcome her resistance? And how much harder it would be to be separated from a newly born infant — supposing she was indeed pregnant — for a matter of conscience which might seem merely theoretical after she had undergone childbirth again.

At this point it may be supposed that Mrs Vavasour, who had advised her own husband 'to cast away all care and fear for her and his children', gave Margaret similar counsel and strengthened her resolve to leave her children's welfare in the hands of God.

Margaret had never felt fit for martyrdom, though she admired it above all earthly things and was prepared to accept it as the will of God. She made a 'voluntary and ready offering of herself to a cruel death in the testimony of her true love to him and the truth of his Catholic faith'. 'When we had been talking of these dangerous times', says Fr Mush, recalling events of the previous year, ' . . . and it hath been told her . . . that if she escaped their bloody hands, yet she should be cast into perpetual prison, she would with smiling countenance wag her head and say, "I pray God his will may be done, and I have that which he seeth most fit for me. But I see not in myself any worthiness of martyrdom; yet, if it be his will, I pray him that I may be constant and persevere to the end.' "

143

The members of the Council who visited her were baffled by her attitude. 'They asked her why she would not so much as desire to be reprieved for some time.' She did not tell them the supernatural reason which filled her with such joy — 'I could but rejoice, my cause also being God's quarrel' — but fell back upon her conviction that whatever she did, they meant to kill her. So she said, 'I require no favour in this matter; you may do your pleasures. . . . You have me now, do your wills.'

They tried to extract evidence from her against 'Ingleby and Mush, the two traitor priests,' but she refused to discuss them. 'I have not to accuse any man,' she said.

Clench had given Margaret a week's respite, and during this time great efforts were made to force her into an act of apostasy. Offers of favour or pardon were dangled before her if only she would 'go to the church . . . if it were but to one sermon'. She asked several times if she might speak with her husband before she died, and this too was made conditional upon her 'yielding unto something'. She replied, 'God's will be done, for I will not offend God and my conscience to speak with him'; so she did not see him again.

Of the many persons who plagued Margaret in her last days, probably one alone appreciated her integrity. Some of them seemed bent on confusing her, by attributing their own opinions to priests whom she had known, saying, for example, that Fr Hart 'said it was lawful for women that had no learning to defend their cause, to go to the church'. They also said 'that Mr Comberford on his death-bed'[5] — he had died in Hull on 4 March — 'renounced the Pope and confessed that he had been blindly led many years'. Margaret answered, 'This is not the first lie that hath been made of dead men, which are not here to answer, but such talk as this will get you small credit.'

Then there was the Puritan, Edmund Bunney, formerly Sub-Dean, now a Prebendary and itinerant preacher, who put questions to her and immediately contradicted their purport. Margaret had been confronted with Bunney long before, at the time of her first imprisonment. He pretended to find her greatly changed from the earlier days when she had, he said, been 'more conformable', and he claimed that she had been influenced to take a firmer stand. His remarks drew from her the exclamation, 'I marvel why you charge me thus: have you found me since the first time I came to prison in any other mind than I am now? Have I not always answered you, that whatsoever the Catholic Church teacheth and believeth, the same I firmly believe? Neither do I shrink any jot from any article thereof, and I trust in my Lord God never to do.'

In the course of both his visits Bunney 'made as it were an oration, and alleged texts of Scriptures', taking her through the controversies of the day, but he merely elicited from Margaret firm professions of faith.

'I am,' she said, 'fully resolved in all things touching my faith, which I ground upon Jesu Christ, and by him I steadfastly believe to be saved, which faith I acknowledge to be the same that he left to his Apostles, and they to their successors from time to time, and is taught in the Catholic Church through all Christendom, and promised to remain with her unto the world's end, and hell-gates shall not prevail against it: and by God's assistance I mean to live and die in the same faith; for if an angel come from heaven, and preach any other doctrine than we have received, the Apostle biddeth us not believe him.'(cf. Gal. 1. 8.)

Bunney was accompanied by Robert Pease—he and Bunney had hurled insults at Fr Hart on the scaffold—and the Puritan James Cottrell,[6] a Dubliner, examiner of witnesses for the Council. Yet another visitor was Richard Harwood, who had been appointed the previous year as preacher for the city, on the recommendation of Henry Cheke. None of these men, who alternately harangued Margaret and stormed at her, were ever able to 'move her to impatience, change of talk or countenance', though several times she begged them to cease troubling her.

When, however, Giles Wigginton visited her again, Margaret seems to have welcomed him. She who 'exceeded in compassion', appreciated that quality in others, and she must have been deeply touched by his charity and courage in interrupting the judge in open court on her behalf, especially as she had dismissed him so curtly the previous night. (Evidently, a certain sharpness of tongue was one of those 'little imperfections' which Fr Mush said 'remained in her'.) Margaret was not, perhaps, aware that Wigginton, vicar of Sedbergh, had himself already suffered at least one term of harsh imprisonment for Calvinist preaching. (He was probably under Huntingdon's protection when he appeared in York in March 1586,[7] for later in the year the Earl was to intercede in vain when he was sentenced to deprivation.) In his simplicity, Wigginton had ignored his own precarious situation and spoken in Margaret's defence; moreover, he had stressed the very point on which she took her stand, the supremacy of the law of God. Clearly his action had softened Margaret's heart towards him — but not her head.

'The third day came Wigginton, the Puritan, and, as they say, he began in this manner:'

> WIGGINTON: Mrs Clitherow, I pity your case. I am sent to see if you will be any whit conformable. Cast not yourself away; lose not both body and soul. Possibly you think you shall have martyrdom, but you are foully deceived, for it cometh but one way. *Not death, but the cause maketh a martyr.* In the time of Queen Mary were many put to death, and now also in this Queen's time, for two several opinions;[8] both these cannot be martyrs. Therefore, good Mistress Clitherow, take pity on yourself. Christ himself fled his persecutors, so did his Apostles; and why should not you then favour your own life?
>
> MARGARET: God defend I should favour my life in this point. As for my martyrdom, I am not yet assured of it, for that I am yet living; but if I persevere to the end, I verily believe I shall be saved. (cf Matt. 10. 22.)
>
> WIGGINTON: Are not you assured?
>
> MARGARET: No, I wis [i.e. indeed], so long as I am living, because I know not what I may do.

146

WIGGINTON: How think you, Mrs Clitherow, to be saved?

MARGARET: Through Christ Jesus his bitter passion and death.

WIGGINTON: You say well, but you believe far otherwise, as in images, ceremonies, sacramentals, sacraments, and such like, and not only in Christ.

MARGARET: I believe as the Catholic Church teacheth me, that there be seven sacraments, and in this faith will I both live and die. As for all the ceremonies, I believe they be ordained to God's honour and glory, and the setting forth of his glory and service; as for images, they be but to represent unto us that there were both good and godly men upon earth, which now are glorious in heaven, and also to stir up our dull minds to more devotion when we behold them; otherwise than thus I believe not.

WIGGINTON: There be not seven sacraments, but two only, that is, Baptism and the Supper of our Lord; as for all the other, they be but ceremonies, good, holy things, but yet not sacraments.

MARGARET: They be all sacraments, ordained by Christ and his Apostles, and all the whole Church hath confirmed them ever since.

WIGGINTON: Well, Mrs Clitherow, I am sorry that I cannot persuade you.

With that he departed. He felt sufficiently encouraged, however, to call on Margaret again a few days later.

WIGGINTON: Mrs Clitherow, I am once again come to you. I am sent by the Council to see if you be any more conformable than you were before. Will you come and hear a godly sermon? Otherwise, I know not how you will escape the danger of the law.

Margaret, in the very shadow of death, teased Wigginton with a kind of affection.

147

MARGARET: I will with all my heart hear a sermon.
WIGGINTON: That is very well said, good Mrs Clitherow.
MARGARET: I pray you understand me. I mind to do it, if
    I may have a Catholic priest or preacher, but to come to
    your sermons I will never.

Wigginton did not understand teasing, especially in such circumstances as these. He tried to press home what he thought to be an advantage he had gained.

WIGGINTON: If you will come to a sermon, I shall
    procure you a good and godly man both of life and
    doctrine, though I seek him to the furthermost part of
    England.

Giles Wigginton was either a very approachable person, or else he failed to command respect, for at this point Mrs Yoward, who was present, interrupted him to suggest to Margaret, 'Here is the Dean of Durham, Toby Matthew, a godly and learned man; I am sure he will take as much pains as any to do you good.'

Margaret answered, mildly, 'I will never have the Dean of Durham, nor any other of that sect; my faith is stayed already, and I purpose not to seek for new doctrine.'

Then Wigginton made a statement which confirms the opinion of the modern Protestant writer who calls him 'quaint'. 'I myself,' he said, 'have seen Christ in a vision, and am assured of my salvation.'

He told Margaret this partly in the hope of gaining her friendship by the exchange of confidences; he wished, too, to impress her by his faith in his own salvation, for he knew that she had no such complete assurance as long as she were alive. Margaret's reaction to his words was that of any normal person, but how far from normal was her situation! She 'began to smile, and made but small answer'.

'Then Wigginton brought forth some places of the Doctors to prove that his doctrine was true.' Margaret, an apt pupil of Fathers Hart and Thirkeld, and as willing to save

Wigginton's soul as he was to save hers, took him up on his sources, saying, 'If you would believe the Doctors and follow them, then were both you and I of one faith, but you slide from them. I have no learning to read them, but I believe that which they preached and taught to be the truth.'

Wigginton realized that to influence Margaret was beyond his power, and as he prepared to leave her, he said with a touch of bitterness at his failure, and annoyance at her obstinacy, 'Well, Mrs Clitherow, I perceive you will cast yourself willingly away, without regard of husband or children; you follow blind guides.'

It occurred to him that he had just been discussing the Doctors of the Church with a butcher's wife who never went to church. Where had she learned about them? Who, in fact, were these 'blind guides' of hers, these priests?

'Is there any of them that hath any learning, I would fain know?' he asked.

But he had hurt Margaret by his suggestion that she did not care for her husband and children. His interest in scholarship seemed an irrelevance. Yes, some of her guides had possessed that kind of learning, but they also had the knowledge and love of God, love which they had proved in their own blood. With a flash of that ready wit of hers, playing on the word 'works', she replied, 'Peruse their works, and you shall see.'

So Giles Wigginton, 'after that he had pitied her case a while, . . . departed and came no more'.

One of the remarkable things about these discussions with Wigginton is the fact that Catholics were not encouraged to 'confer' with Protestants, as readiness to do so was usually interpreted as a sign of wavering. Margaret, of course, did not engage in a formal disputation, but she was more ready to discuss religion with Wigginton, who had proved his sincerity, and who knew when to leave her, than she was with those whom she mistrusted and who would not go away when she asked them. In the discussions with Wigginton may be seen a glimpse of Margaret at work as the apostle who 'had a vehement desire that all others . . . might know

God and his truth', and who 'let no occasion slip, no opportunity escape, to draw all with whom she might safely deal
. . .'

Among the kinsfolk, 'both men and women', who came to
beg Margaret to consider her husband and children was no
less a personage than Henry May, Lord Mayor of York.
Henry, as much as anyone, was affected by the miscarriage
of the plan to terrify Margaret into conformity. So far from
beginning his period of office with the distinction of winning
back his stepdaughter to the established church, he had been
dismayed to watch her taking up a position which, whatever
the outcome, would bring shame upon himself and the
Council. Now they must either retract their threats and
spare her life without making her conform, or see that a
sentence was carried out which was so barbarous as to stir up
public opinion against the Council still further.

Henry May could visit Margaret without the ignominy of
being seen to enter the prison, for the Lord Mayor's office
was in the same building, next to the Council Chamber. He
had himself been a member of the committee appointed the
previous year 'to view the chambers in the chapel . . . that
order may be taken . . . for more strait keeping of the
prisoners there'.

Margaret looked up from her prayers and found her stepfather standing before her, sadly shaking his head. For
twelve years he had battled to regain such control as he once
had of her conscience; now the last duel was to take place.

Henry May, then, 'kneeling down on his knees, as they
say, with great show of sorrow and affection, by all flattery
allured her to do something against her conscience . . . and
he would not doubt yet to get her pardon. . . . She valiantly
resisted. And when he perceived that nothing would serve,
he desired her to give him her eldest daughter. . . . She was
loath her child should be infected with his heresy' so 'she
thanked him, and refused his courtesy'.

Had he really cared for Margaret, Henry May might have
appealed to Lady Huntingdon to intercede with her husband;

150

she had once successfully pleaded for Dr Vavasour to be let out of prison to visit his sick wife. But this action would have been deeply humiliating to Mr May, and would have affected his standing with the Lord President. He left the prison raging, and 'made this his honourable table talk among his . . . brethren, that she died desperately' — that is, that she was bent on this death as a form of suicide — 'and that she had been an unhonest [i.e. immoral] woman, with many such like false . . . slanders.'[9] Margaret's real offence was to disgrace him at the very height of his achievement, and, moreover, to make him look foolish and ineffectual before the Council.

He need not have feared that he would lose the favour of the Earl of Huntingdon; the Earl's shoulders were broad enough to bear the responsibility for Margaret's death, which ultimately rested with him, and he had until that time been no more lenient towards women recusants than towards men. Henry May's finest hour was only five months away.

Margaret Clitherow was accustomed to the necessity of balancing her duty to God against her duty to the State and against her duty to her husband, but the most painful decision she had to take concerned her children. She always denied that she was 'casting herself away' — 'I die not desperately,' she said, 'nor willingly procure mine own death' — or that she 'had no care on her husband and children, but would spoil [i.e. was willing to ruin] them'. 'As for my husband,' she said, 'know you that I love him next unto God in this world, and I have care over my children as a mother ought to have; I trust I have done my duty to them to bring them up in the fear of God, and so *I trust now I am discharged of them*. And for this cause I am willing to offer them freely to God that sent them to me, rather than I will yield one jot from my faith. I confess death is fearful, and flesh is frail; yet I mind by God's assistance to spend my blood in this faith, as willing as ever I put my paps to my children's mouths, neither desire I to have my death deferred.'

Margaret had already been well schooled in detachment from her children by her years in prison. She had, too, offered her son Henry freely to God when she sent him abroad, and she well knew that her children's constancy in the Faith depended upon her own. But what did those words cost her in human suffering? If ever a woman loved her children *in Christ* it was this one, and two at least did their utmost to follow the example of her life. It had been the will of God that she should bear them; now he had expressed his will in another way. He had an even higher task for her than their upbringing: to die for him. She obeyed, but her action was above nature, and incomprehensible to her visitors.

In a final effort to move her they repeated the slanders that Henry May was publishing. They 'urged her to confess she had offended her husband'. They 'told her how the boy had confessed that she had sinned with priests, and that the priests and she would have delicate cheer, when she would set her husband with bread and butter and a red herring. When she heard these words, she *smiled* and said: "God forgive you for these forged tales; and if the boy said so" ' — and she seemed to doubt it — ' "I warrant you he will say as much more for a pound of figs." . . . "If I have offended my husband in anything but for my conscience, I ask God and him forgiveness . . . I trust my husband will not accuse me that I have offended him at any time, unless in such small matters as are commonly incident to man and wife." '

So Margaret Clitherow continued in prison for ten days after her sentence, calm, composed, natural, able to smile as usual at the ridiculous, even while she was being slandered, 'never expecting or hoping for pardon notwithstanding the time was so deferred, and many speeches given forth that she should not die. But her mind was always on her end, craving all good prayers for perseverance and for ghostly strength to overcome all combats, and joyfully to depart this world to the glory of God and advancement of the Catholic Church.'

To the last she was an apostle.

XV

Martyrdom

MARGARET'S composure was put to the test during the second week of her imprisonment on the bridge. At the weekend 'her husband was set at liberty, and commanded by the Council to depart the city for five days'. This was the first intimation, which soon reached Margaret, that they intended to carry out the sentence.

On the Tuesday night the sheriffs of York, Fawcett and Gibson, 'came to her and told her what day was appointed for her death'; it was the following Friday, the first day that the Council would be free of Clench's prohibition. They did not wait to see whether they would meanwhile 'hear from him to the contrary', as he had bid them, for their minds were made up.

When the sheriffs brought the news to Margaret, she 'thanked God, and requested them that she might go to the place where she should suffer half a day or half a night before, and to remain there all that time until she should die; but they would not grant it'. She may still have thought that the place of her death would be the Knavesmire, already hallowed by the martyrs, for Fr Mush reports also that she asked to be taken there, 'to suffer what cruelty they pleased', but was refused.

'After the sheriffs were departed, the martyr said to a friend of hers' — Mrs Vavasour, perhaps — ' "The sheriffs have told me that I shall die on Friday next; and now I feel the frailty of mine own flesh, which trembleth at these news, although my spirit greatly rejoiceth. Therefore for God's sake pray for me, and desire all good folks to do the same." And she kneeling down praying a little, the fear and horror of death presently [i.e. immediately] departed, as she said herself.'

This was the only occasion when she 'showed herself sad, or sorrowful, or fearful'. Yet until the last she would not in any way rely upon her own strength, remembering always that 'death is fearful, and flesh is frail'. 'My spirit is very willing, although my flesh may repine,' she said. 'Flesh is frail, but I trust in my Lord Jesu, that he will give me strength to bear all troubles and torments which shall be laid upon me for his sake.'

From the time that the sheriffs brought her this information 'she took no food at all'. In this way, whether deliberately or not, she carried out a part of her sentence that was not imposed upon her: she continued 'three days without meat or drink'.

She occupied herself in these last few days with an important piece of needlework. She must have asked Mrs Vavasour to obtain a piece of linen for her, about the time that she heard her husband had been sent away, and with it she who had always been 'quick in the dispatch of business' made 'a linen habit like to an alb . . . to suffer martyrdom in'.

Margaret had two purposes in view in making this garment; one was symbolic, for her mind at this time dealt in symbols. The making of this white garment reveals her heart more clearly than words can say. Another Yorkshire martyr, the great St John Fisher, had taken the same action fifty years earlier. On the morning of his execution he asked his manservant 'to lay him out a clean white shirt, and all the best apparel he had as cleanly brushed as might be', and to his enquiry replied, 'Dost thou not mark that this is our marriage day, and that it behoveth us therefore to use more cleanliness for solemnity of that marriage?'[1]

It is the symbolism of the Apocalypse: 'For the marriage of the Lamb is come: and his wife hath prepared herself. And it is granted to her that she should clothe herself with fine linen, glittering and white. For the fine linen are the justifications of saints. And he said to me: Write: Blessed are they

154

that are called to the marriage supper of the Lamb' (Apoc. 19, 7-9).

It was in order to be sure of a clean white garment to die in that Margaret had 'put off her smock' when she first came to this prison; she did not put it on again until the morning of her death. (By the end of the first day of the Assizes she had accepted death; this was evident from her frankness in referring to priests on the second day.) She did not know, when she came to the prison on the bridge, what her sentence was to be, and when it was passed next day she heard that she was to die naked. Either she knew, or she guessed, that so long as her legs were bare her executioners would be satisfied. So her second, practical, reason for making the 'habit' was to give her the minimum of covering, and she made it just long enough to cover her body. It was, however, most important that the garment should have long sleeves.

Few people if condemned to be hanged would think of providing the rope themselves. Margaret Clitherow, who was 'very willing' to die, provided part of the apparatus required for the carrying out of her sentence: to the sleeves of her 'habit' she evidently sewed tapes[2] 'to bind her hands'. She felt she was 'unworthy of so good a death as this is', but she was not going to miss dying with arms outstretched like her Saviour, since he had so wonderfully given her this privilege.

Still acting symbolically, with the heightened perception of her last days, 'her hat before she died she sent to her husband, in sign of her loving duty to him as to her head. Her hose and shoes to her eldest daughter, Anne . . . , signifying that she should serve God and follow her steps of virtue.'

The account of Margaret's last night on earth shows with what affection she was now regarded by the Protestant Mrs Yoward.

'Being in a parlour with Yoward and his wife the night before she suffered, she said to Yoward's wife, "I would gladly have one of the maids to bear me company this night, not for any fear of death, for it is my comfort, but the flesh is frail." '

'The maids' may well have been Mrs Vavasour's two young daughters, Anne and Dorothy, who were also in this prison.[3]

'The woman said, "Alas! Mrs Clitherow, the gaoler is gone, the door is locked, and none can be had."

'Then the said Yoward's wife, being ready to go to bed, clasped [i.e. fastened] again her clothes, and kneeling beside the martyr till almost midnight, after went to bed. At twelve of the clock' — there was a chiming clock in the steeple of St William's Chapel, which was overhead — 'she saw the martyr rise from her knees, and put off all her apparel,' putting on the linen habit. 'Then she kneeled down again, without anything upon her saving that linen cloth, from twelve of the clock until three, at which time she arose and came to the fireside. There she laid her down flat upon the stones one quarter of an hour.'

(Again, whether deliberately or not, Margaret was carrying out part of her sentence: she was to return to the prison, and *there* be stripped naked and laid down, her back upon the ground. . . .)

'After that she arose and went to her bed, covering herself with clothes, and so continued until six in the morning. Then she arose and put on her apparel, and made her ready against the sheriffs' coming.'

Though Margaret had sent her hat to her husband, she still had the linen or woollen coif without which a married woman never appeared in public. But she was 'called to the marriage supper of the Lamb', and so she went bareheaded; she 'trimmed up her head with new inkle [i.e. tape]', a substitute for the silks and ribbons which had adorned her hair when she went to her marriage with John Clitherow. It was as a bride that she stepped out of the New Counter prison.

'She desired Yoward's wife to see her die, and wished her that some good Catholics were by, in her last agony and pains of death, to put her in remembrance of God. Yoward's wife said she would not see her die so cruel a death for all York; "but," quoth she, "I will procure some friends to lay weight on you that you may be quickly dispatched from your pain".

'The martyr said, "No, good Mrs Yoward, not so. God defend that I should procure any to be guilty of my death and blood."

'About eight of the clock the sheriffs came to her, and she being ready expecting them, . . . carrying on her arm the new habit of linen with inkle strings . . . went cheerfully to her marriage, as she called it; dealing her alms in the street, which was so full of people that she could scarce pass by them.'

The streets would be full of people this day in any case, for this was one of the holy days when all were obliged to go to church: the Feast of the Annunciation of the Blessed Virgin Mary, which was also the first day of the new Year of Grace, 1586, as it was then reckoned.

'She went barefoot and barelegged, her gown loose about her.

'Fawcett, the sheriff, made haste and said, "Come away, Mrs Clitherow."

'The martyr answered merrily, "Good Master Sheriff, let me deal my poor alms before I now go, for my time is but short."

'They marvelled all to see her joyful countenance.

'The place of execution was the Tollbooth, six or seven yards distant from the prison.' This was the office of the collector of bridge tolls. It stood across the road from the prison, and was the last building on the bridge at the Micklegate end. Other accounts indicate that it was open to the street, but had rooms inside, and that Margaret was taken into 'a close house'. At one period the Corporation had held its meetings in this building.

Here, where the severed head of Thomas Percy had once lain, Margaret Clitherow came to die.

'There were present at her martyrdom the two sheriffs of

157

York, Fawcett and Gibson, Frost, a minister, Fox, Mr Cheke's kinsman, with another of his men, the four sergeants, which had hired certain beggars to do the murder, three or four men, and four women.

'The martyr coming to the place, kneeled her down, and prayed to herself. The tormentors bade her pray with them, and they would pray with her.'

They were still hoping for some act that could be construed as apostasy, not that it would save her life now, but because they needed a little victory to use as propaganda and to offset their shame. So they would intrude even into her converse with God, to confuse her last moments. Who should say, if they prayed with her, that she was not praying with them?

Clear-headed to the last, 'the martyr denied, and said, "I will not pray with you, and you shall not pray with me; neither will I say Amen to your prayers, nor shall you to mine."

'Then they willed her to pray for the Queen's Majesty.'

This was intended as a trap. If she refused, she was a traitor; if she prayed they could and would pray with her. But Margaret Clitherow's ready wit did not fail her even now.

'The martyr began in this order. First, in the hearing of them all, she prayed for the Catholic Church, then for the Pope's Holiness, Cardinals, and other Fathers that have charge of souls, and then for all Christian princes. At which words the tormentors interrupted her, and willed her not to put her Majesty among that company; yet the martyr proceeded in this order, "and especially for Elizabeth, Queen of England, that God turn her to the Catholic faith, and that after this mortal life she may receive the blessed joys of heaven. For I wish as much good," quoth she, "to her Majesty's soul as to mine own."'

Gibson, the junior sheriff, who had not been conspicuously active all along, now found himself unable to face Margaret's last moments as the law required of him. He, 'abhorring the cruel fact [i.e. deed], stood weeping at the door. Then said Fawcett, "Mrs Clitherow, you must remember and confess that you die for treason."

'The martyr answered, "No, no, Master Sheriff, I die for the love of my Lord Jesu;" which last words she spake with a loud voice.

'Then Fawcett commanded her to put off her apparel; "For you must die," said he, "naked, as judgement was given and pronounced against you."

'The martyr with the other women requested him on their knees that she might die in her smock, and that for the honour of womanhood they would not see her naked; but that would not be granted. Then she requested that women might unapparel her, and that they would turn their faces from her for that time.

'The women took off her clothes, and put upon her the habit of linen. Then very quickly[4] she laid her down upon the ground, her face covered with a handkerchief, and secret parts with the habit, all the rest of her body being naked. The door was laid upon her. . . . '

And at this moment of horror, terror, and loneliness, Margaret Clitherow no longer seems the far-off saint facing death with incredible fortitude. Suddenly she is a weak, fearful human being like the rest, as she had known herself to be all along. After a night of spiritual preparation she had desired to have some Catholics near her at this moment, 'to put her in remembrance of God'. How shrewd her judgement was! For having provided the tapes to bind her hands so that she would die with arms outstretched, now that she had come to it, she forgot all about this desire, and only knew her need for God's grace. 'Her hands,' says Fr Mush, 'she joined towards her face.' There was no voluntary stretching out of her arms.

'Then the sheriff said, "Nay, you must have your hands bound."

'The martyr put forth her hands over the door still joined' in the attitude of prayer.

'The two sergeants parted them, and with the inkle strings, which she had prepared for that purpose, bound

159

them to two posts, so that her body and her arms made a perfect cross.

'They willed her again to ask the Queen's Majesty's forgiveness, and to pray for her. The martyr said she had prayed for her. They also willed her to ask her husband's forgiveness' — even now they implied her stepfather's slander. 'The martyr said, "If ever I have offended him, but for my conscience, I ask him forgiveness."

'After this they laid weight upon her, which when she first felt, she said, "Jesu! Jesu! Jesu! have mercy on me!" which were the last words she was heard to speak.

'She was in dying one quarter of an hour. A sharp stone, as much as a man's fist, was put under her back; upon her was laid to the quantity of seven or eight hundredweight at the least, which, breaking her ribs, caused them to burst forth of the skin.

' . . . This was at nine of the clock, and she continued in the press until three at afternoon.'

And one of the ancients answered and said to me: These that are clothed in white robes, who are they? And whence are they? And I said to him: My Lord, thou knowest. And he said to me: These are they who are come out of great tribulation and have washed their robes and have made them white in the blood of the Lamb. Therefore, they are before the throne of God: and they serve him day and night in his temple. And he that sitteth on the throne shall dwell over them. They shall no more hunger nor thirst: neither shall the sun fall on them, nor any heat. For the Lamb, which is in the midst of the throne, shall rule them and shall lead them to the fountains of the waters of life: and God shall wipe away all tears from their eyes.

Apocalypse 7. 13-17

XVI

Comment

THE editor of the 1619 *Abstract* of Fr Mush's work, addressing St Margaret's daughter in a long dedicatory notice, says, 'I do not read of a more heroical act performed by any either in our time or many ages before, than this of your Mother'. Her death invites comparison with the deaths of Saints Perpetua and Felicity at Carthage in A.D. 203.

The modern reader, however, has difficulty in understanding Saint Margaret Clitherow, especially her refusal of trial; indeed, this is no new problem, for the two contemporary explanations differ. Margaret *put herself* in a position from which only apostasy could have extricated her. The judge had already stretched a point in uttering the sanction conditionally: 'this must be your judgement, unless you put yourself to be tried'. He said she was unlikely to be found guilty on the slender evidence of one child. (Margaret, however, knew more about the situation in York than he did.)

Had she pleaded and been found guilty, she would have been offered her life as a reward for going to church and hearing a sermon. (She was practically offered her life on these terms even after the supposedly irreversible sanction had been uttered.) Had she refused to conform in these circumstances, and been hanged, like St Margaret Ward and St Anne Line a few years later, there would have been no ambiguity about the way in which she came to her death. As it is, she laid herself open to the charge of suicide, which in fact her stepfather and others brought against her.

She had spent many years refining her conscience; she had also had experience of pleading 'Not guilty' in the court of Quarter Sessions. The jury found her guilty. Among the members of this special jury a few still stand out as individuals: Francis Bayne, mercer, the foreman (with a recusant brother; recusant himself by 1586), William Wood, capper (brother-in-law of Anne Tesh, suspected of sheltering papists himself), William Gilming (innholder, whose daughter Edith was to marry Philip Turner in 1590 and to become an ancestress of Alexander Pope), Robert Watter (hatter and haberdasher, alderman in 1590, Lord Mayor, knighted by King James I in 1603 as he passed through York; his monument survives in the parish room on the site of Holy Cross church). . . . These, too, were people, with souls to be saved. Margaret may have grieved for them after her condemnation on that occasion, but they had sent her to her Catholic retreat in the Castle, not to her death. The Assize jury was another matter; she was convinced that they were bound to find her guilty to please the Council (now grown so over-mighty in the North), and so would 'damnably' offend God.

If Margaret Clitherow's conscience was so sensitive on this point, why were the consciences of Margaret Ward and Anne Line less sensitive? The answer may be that both of these women were tried *in London*, by far the largest and always the most anonymous of cities; it would be extremely unlikely that either would have recognized a single face among the jury, whose individual responsibility was submerged in its brief corporate legal existence. But Margaret's jury were people known to her.

It was to protect other people that she died, whether her servants and children and members of the jury, from certain lifelong regret and possible damnation, or her weaker next-door neighbours, from arraignment on the same charge. (So dangerous was the situation that, writing a few weeks later, Fr Mush tried to divert the attention of his readers from the circumstances, urging that they should 'rather with great diligence endeavour to imitate this her first martyrdom of a

162

virtuous life . . . than curiously to know in what sort she obtained the second of a glorious death'.) At the very end, she said, 'I die for the love of my Lord Jesu.' It was in him that she loved her neighbour, her friend, and she laid down her life for him.

It has also been objected that St Margaret deliberately put her children's future, both material and spiritual, at risk by her action. She could be sure they would not suffer materially; she knew that John would remarry, as every respectable widower did, and they would be well looked after. As for their souls' health: she had instructed them (with evident success in the two cases we know of), she had taught them to pray with her, and placed before them the ideal of martyrdom as the most glorious of privileges. Had she refused that privilege for herself, it is unlikely that any of them would have persevered. She set them an incomparable example of integrity. That she had a true and natural love for them is shown by her statement that she died for Christ 'as willing as ever I put my paps to my children's mouths'.

But in fact all is obscure in this region: we have no more knowledge of how the lives of most of her children worked out, than she herself had of their future. So many early parish registers having been lost, we cannot even identify her children, other than the two we know to have kept the Faith. Possibly one or two of the married women recusants of the next generation were her daughters. The butcher, John Clitherow junior, was not a recusant, but whether he was the son of Margaret or of John's third wife, we simply do not know; from his likely age — he was made free in 1607, and the Butchers' Company insisted on seven years' apprenticeship — it is more probable that he was not Margaret's son.

To say that Margaret loved her neighbour as much as she loved her children sounds very strange, even when the context is the Mystical Body of Christ. But is not the strangeness a measure of our own dullness of heart, our shrinking from the stark simplicity of the Gospel? He who said, 'If you love me, keep my commandments' (John 14. 15), also said, 'He that loveth father or mother more than me, is not worthy of me; and he that loveth son or daughter more than me, is not worthy of me' (Mat. 10. 37); and more forcibly still, 'If any man come to me, and hate not his father, and mother, and wife, and children, and brethren, and sisters, yea and his own life also, he cannot be my disciple. And whosoever doth not carry his cross and come after me, cannot be my disciple' (Luke 14. 26-7).

'But she knowing how precious a gift and benefit of God it was to suffer for his cause any cross, she was also willing it should be imparted to others, and would no less be joyful of their patience than of her own, ever praying for their perseverance to the end.' Fr Mush's words point to the source of some of Margaret's statements in court.

There are other seeming oddities about St Margaret Clitherow, her behaviour in prison during the last week of her life, for instance. But Fr Mush has given us the clue by stressing her desire to obey the will of God in the smallest detail. During the whole of her life as a Catholic, she lived out the message of Salvation history already developed and emphasized in the mystery plays that must have had some effect upon her childhood and that of her contemporaries. Love and obedience to God's salvific will are inevitably and closely related. Margaret Clitherow, in her singleness of heart, accepted the terrible sanction decreed against her as the expression of the will of God, just as she had learned, following the recommended practice of the age, to accept her confessor's decisions.

Her response was the total abandonment of her will to God's. The actions in prison that have seemed so unintelligible to us were messages meant for him. The refusal to eat or drink for three days, the lying on her back upon the hearth, the provision of tapes to ensure that her hands were bound, all in accordance with the judge's sentence, were the answers of her heart: *'Be it done to me according to thy word.'*

She did more than accept death; she went forward to embrace it, since come it must, joyfully, in the spirit already traditional among the English Martyrs. 'Lo, dost thou not see, Meg,' St Thomas More had said to Margaret Roper as the Carthusian martyrs were dragged from the Tower, 'that these blessed fathers be now as cheerfully going to their deaths as bridegrooms to their marriage?' In the same spirit, Margaret Clitherow tied up her hair on that spring morning and took up the white garment she had made for her 'marriage'. Her attitude, even more than that of the martyred priests who used similar expressions, is a forcible reminder of the Church's mystical theology of marriage.

We cannot thoroughly analyse another human being, least of all one who so fully corresponded with grace as St Margaret did. Let us give her the last words: 'I die for the love of my Lord Jesu.' And also, 'Make of it what you will, I pass not.'[1]

XVII

Aftermath

I T was not long before Fr Mush, in his rage and grief, was claiming that the arraignment had been illegal, for it was established practice that an accessory should not be tried before a principal. Fr Francis Ingleby, named in the indictment, was still at large when the Assizes were held.

Though it may be argued that the statute of 27 Elizabeth made the harbourer into a principal, the Earl of Huntingdon was, after his death, accredited with having for many years been content to take 'secret intelligence' of such persons and not to bring them to trial or execution (at least by the Council) 'unless there were a seminary taken'.[1] The penal laws were in fact very elastic, useful tools for the government to have in hand. For example, in 1590, when anti-Catholic feeling was less intense, the assault by the Spanish Armada which had been feared for so long having entirely failed, a York merchant, Thomas Maskew, who had evidently committed the 'felony' of harbouring a priest, was merely put on bond not to do so again![2]

Yet another case, however, in 1594, was to show Huntingdon treating a female 'harbourer' with no more clemency than the Council had proposed for Margaret Clitherow. Grace Claxton had been condemned to death at Durham Assizes; she claimed the benefit of the *venter* and was at first refused it because, it was said, she should have claimed it before judgement. Huntingdon, obliged to explain his actions fully to Lord Burghley, reversed his decision in order 'to stop the mouths of those that incline always falsely to slander the mercy and justice of this happy and gracious government'.[3] (In this case, clemency proved the better policy: Grace Claxton apostatized.)

Had the Queen known of Margaret's condemnation, there is no doubt she would have intervened, even if a constitutional problem had arisen concerning the limits of the President's powers. In 1598 she robbed Mrs. Wiseman of the palm of martyrdom in the same circumstances. Hearing how 'for so small a matter she should have been put to death', the Queen 'rebuked the justices of cruelty, and said she should not die'.[4] There are several other instances of her distress at the execution of a woman. (It may be no coincidence that John Clench, whom Queen Elizabeth had called her 'good judge', never received a knighthood, nor, apparently, any other honour, although he lived to be the oldest judge of his time.)

The Privy Council, in Mrs. Wiseman's case, had already given a stay of execution, not wishing 'to shock London by their barbarity'.[5] In 1596, Margaret's friend Anne Tesh, and Bridget Maskew (wife of Thomas), having been betrayed, while in prison, by an *agent provocateur*, a minister who pretended a great desire to become a Catholic, were sentenced to be burned to death. On the intervention of friends at court, the sentences were commuted to life imprisonment, and on the accession of King James I they were released. When the political situation was easier, mercy had more chance to prevail.

By the time that Fr Mush wrote his *True Report*, in the early summer of 1586, he had helped to find and dispose of Saint Margaret's body; this fact, revealed in an early seventeenth-century manuscript copy of his book in the Vatican Library,[6] adds to the poignancy and psychological interest of his work.

The sheriffs' sergeants had been ordered to bury the body at midnight 'in an obscure and filthy corner of the city . . . which they did with great secrecy. . . . Her ghostly father and others being desirous to have the sacred body reserved with some due honour laboured all they could to find it and when they had sought divers places at last it was found the same Friday six weeks after she had been buried. They took it up by night and carried it on horseback a far journey from York and within four or five days prepared spices and with reverence buried it again where with God's grace it may be kept a glorious relic for better times to come.' The body was incorrupt, 'without any ill smell. . . .'[7] Its present resting-place is unknown. The Bar Convent, York, possesses the relic of a hand, traditionally said to be Saint Margaret's; there was once a relic of her hair at Westminster Cathedral.[8]

The fate of many of the other people concerned in this tragic and glorious story is known. We have mentioned the sentence passed upon Anne Tesh in 1596; in the summer of 1586 she was brought out from the Castle, where she had shared a room with Margaret, and tried on a charge of harbouring, the wretched Flemish boy having been brought to accuse her, although he did not know her by sight, and she lived in a distant parish. The jury courageously found her Not guilty of harbouring a priest, but Guilty of hearing Mass, for which she was fined. She continued recusant.

In 1587, Mrs Vavasour, Mary Hutton (wife of William Hutton, the 'Prisoner in Ouse Bridge Kidcote') and Alice Oldcorne, suspected of having been accessories to the theft of the heads of some martyred priests from the leads of St William's Chapel, near their prison, were transferred to the 'low prison' at the river level. Here they all caught an infection from which they rapidly died.[9]

John Clitherow remarried, probably quite soon. With the loss of his recusant wife, he became respectable again. In 1589 he was chosen trustee for a Butchers' charity. In 1603 he was among the 'best citizens and inhabitants' to meet King James on his journey from Scotland. He was almost certainly still alive in 1614. His life was not, however, free from trouble even after his wife's death. In 1589 or there-abouts, his daughter Anne ran away from home, and by July 1593 she was in Lancaster Gaol, for causes ecclesiastical.[10] She entered St Ursula's Convent, Louvain, in 1596, and was professed as an Augustinian Canoness Regular of the Lateran in 1598. She 'followed well her holy mother's virtuous steps, for she was a very good religious, who set herself seriously to the ways of perfection, . . . she laboured well in the overcoming of her nature and the practice of solid virtue. She also by her own industry got the Latin tongue so well as to understand it perfectly. . . . She also assisted . . . much in the erection of' St Monica's, Louvain, which was opened for English nuns in 1611, although she was unable to go there herself, because 'she wanted friends to allow her means.' She died in August 1622, leaving behind 'much edification of virtue and also note of sanctity'.[11] (Her unique copy of the *Abstract* of Fr Mush's *True Report*, published in 1619, has survived in the possession of her community, now at Newton Abbot, Devon.)

Henry Clitherow never became a priest. By December 1588 he was a student at the English College, Rheims; in October 1590 he was at the English College, Rome. He then tried his vocation among the Capuchin Franciscans, in 1592, but transferred to the Dominicans at some time, dying at Viterbo at an unknown date, *mente motus* (which could mean either that he was mentally disturbed, or that he had changed his mind).[12]

Millicent Calvert, John Clitherow's sister, did not appear in the official lists of recusants again, but about the year 1593, a boy named John Jackson met a 'sister of Mrs Clitherow' in York; she 'told him much about priests, but refused to reveal their whereabouts because, as she said, he was young and the times were dangerous. . . .'[13] Margaret's sister Alice Hutchinson is not known as a recusant at any period, so it is likely that her sister-in-law was the woman concerned.

Henry May, after his term of office as Lord Mayor, had the humiliation of falling into debt. (The expenses of the mayoralty were notorious.) In list after list his name appears as owing money. At one stage, the Corporation ingeniously assisted him by taking a lease of his house in St Saviourgate for a knitting factory employing pauper children. His step-son George Middleton appears to have bought some of the properties he occupied in Coney Street and Davygate and to have gradually sold them back to him; the last payment of £50 was still outstanding at his death. He continued, however, to purchase other house property, some for development. He bequeathed to George Middleton his best black gown guarded with velvet and faced with 'fynes', to John Clitherow the gold signet that he wore on his little finger, and to his brother Roger his long black cloak. Alderman Thomas Jackson was one of the supervisors of his will.[14]

Margaret's elder stepson, William, and his brother Thomas, a draper, were presented together to the High Commission, on recusancy charges, in December 1599; William remained at large as an obstinate recusant, but Thomas was committed to close prison in York Castle, dying in the Hull Blockhouse in March 1603. Thereupon, in May 1604, William went to the English College, Douai, and was ordained priest in March 1608, being sent on the English mission in August of that year. He seems to have been imprisoned several times, but died at Brandsby in 1636, as chaplain to the Cholmely family.[15]

Margaret's prayers for her son Henry were answered in a different fashion. By the time Fr Mush wrote his *True Report*, Brian Stapleton, her children's schoolmaster, was safely out of the country; he would not otherwise have identified him. A man of that name, of the diocese of York, arrive at Rheims on 14 June 1586, was ordained priest on 19 September 1587, and sent to England about October 1590. He was in the North in 1593.[16] That was evidently one man's reaction to Margaret's death. As for Fr John Mush, though said to have been imprisoned several times, he died in his bed in 1617.

When we turn to the descendants of some of the persons involved in the death of St Margaret Clitherow — enemies for whom she prayed — a remarkable pattern emerges. Henry May's second wife had given him three sons and a daughter; sons Edward (born in October 1586) and Henry (born in April 1588) survived. Admonished to bring up their children in the fear of God and in learning, the Lady Anne May, six months after Henry's death, married a Catholic,

Gabriel Thwaites, a younger son of John Thwaites, esquire, of Marston. Within a year, Gabriel Thwaites appeared at the city Quarter Sessions as a recusant; by 1613 both of Henry May's sons, also Edward May's wife, were non-communicant and negligent comers to church, and Edward's younger children were not baptized at his parish church, St Martin's.[17]

The third Earl of Huntingdon had no children. The man who, in the absence of the Earl, may have been personally responsible, in the last resort, for not exercising the prerogative of clemency for Margaret Clitherow, was Lord Evers, or Eure. In 1626 his grandson is said to have been a 'convict popish recusant',[18] and his great-grandson Ralph Eure also died a recusant in 1640.[19]

The male line of Francis Rodes's descendants failed; the house that he built at Barlborough is now a Jesuit preparatory school, and a room containing a flamboyant fireplace with figures and arms of himself and his two wives is a chapel in which daily Mass is said.

This is interesting, but the history of the female line of descendants of Francis Rodes is startling. In 1626 his granddaughter Lennox Rodes married Marmaduke Langdale, who in 1658 became the first Baron Langdale of Holme on Spalding Moor. (Her mother, Frances, daughter of Marmaduke Constable of Wassand in the parish of Sigglesthorne, the third wife of Sir John Rodes, had previously, in 1585 at the church of St Michael le Belfrey, York, married that same Henry Cheke, who as Secretary to the Council in the North took part in Margaret's arraignment. On his death she married the son of his friend Francis Rodes.[20])

The first Baron Langdale is thought to have become a Catholic; his son certainly did, and through him the Catholic descendants of Francis Rodes may be traced, men and women who for generations founded and endowed missions, built and maintained chapels, paid double Land Tax, accepted their inability to hold public office or to sit in the House of Lords, sent their children abroad for their education and produced innumerable priests and nuns. Their contribution towards the rebuilding of the Catholic Church in England has been incalculable. They included the saintly layman, Charles Langdale, who fought in the Victorian Parliament for Catholic rights lost in the Elizabethan, and also the sixteenth Duke of Norfolk, by descent through his mother.

Saint Margaret Clitherow died, she said, 'to God's glory and the advancement of his Catholic Church'. Four hundred years later we can look back upon the history of the Church in England since her death, and see, if we will, a large area of it as directly resulting, not merely from the inspiration of her life and death, but from the intercession of the Martyrs for their enemies and their descendants. The future lay with those who prayed, not with those who plotted.

Fr Mush, towards the end of his *True Report*, asks Margaret's 'murderers', 'Can your own blood or your posterity's wash away the reproach of this same turpitude?'[21] We cannot keep Heaven's balance-sheet, but looking back from this distance of time, for ourselves we may judge that the rancour of the martyrdoms has been washed out, leaving only the joy. As Gregory Martin wrote in his preface to the Rheims New Testament: 'We repine not in tribulation but ever love them that hate us, pitying their case and rejoicing in our own. For neither we see during this life how much good they do us, nor know how many of them shall be (as we heartily desire they all may be) saved: our Lord and Saviour having paid the same price by his death for them and for us. Love all, therefore, pray for all'.

Abbreviations

AJ	*Ampleforth Journal*
BIHR	Borthwick Institute of Historical Research
BL	British Library
CRS	Catholic Record Society
QS	Quarter Sessions
Rec.Hist.	*Recusant History*
SS	Surtees Society
VCH	*Victoria County History*
YAS	Yorkshire Archaeological Society
YCA	York City Archives
YCR	*York Civic Records*
YML	York Minster Library
YPL	York (Central) Public Library (Reference Dept.)

Documentation

I

1 BIHR: Wills 11, f. 104v.
2 id., f. 465v.
3 BIHR: CP G1331.
4 BIHR: D/C Wills 5, f. 9r-v.
5 BIHR: Wills 11, f. 267v.
6 YAS rec. ser. xlv, 24, 28, 35.
7 R. Davies, *Pope: additional facts concerning his maternal ancestry* (1858), 7–9.
8 BIHR: Wills 21, ff. 416r–417v.
9 Davies, op. cit.; J. Hunter, *Pope: his descent and family connections: facts and conjectures* (1857); V. Rumbold, 'Alexander Pope and the religious tradition of the Turners' (in *Rec. Hist.*, vol. 17, no. 1, May 1984. I do not, however, accept the assumptions of this article. K.M.L.) For outline pedigree, see App.IV below.
10 BIHR: Wills 17, f. 661r-v.
11 Nor have the parents of the York priest-martyr Robert Middleton (d.1601) been identified.

II

1 The late Mr Stanley Bell, sometime head verger of York Minster and churchwarden of St Michael le Belfrey church, first drew my attention to this amazing stone, the underside of which he had had an opportunity to examine. Dr Eric Gee has confirmed that it is an altar-stone; Dr Christopher Wilson has identified its material. K.M.L.
2 BIHR: PR. Y/MCS 16 (Churchwardens' accounts of St Martin, Coney St., vol. 1).

3 C. Cross, 'Lay literacy and clerical misconduct in a York parish during the reign of Mary Tudor' (in *York Historian*, no. 3, 1980, 10–15). This child, born *c*.1554, may have been the Elizabeth Middleton buried at St Martin's on 7 Nov. 1557; or it could have been Margaret herself. It is curious to reflect that the Pearl of York might have been invalidly baptized, though, as the stipendiary priest of St Martin's, William Mottey (SS xcii, 461–2) was also present on this occasion, he would presumably have given the child a valid private baptism afterwards. In any case, martyrdom ('baptism by blood') confers the same grace.

4 BIHR: CP. G1331.

III

1 BIHR: Wills 17, f. 661r–v.

2 See App. IIIa for an explanation of the discrepancies in dating between my *Margaret Clitherow* and the present work. Henry May was made free in 1567, not 1566; to judge from the position of his name in the original Freemen's Register (YCA, D1), he obtained his freedom at about the time of his marriage. K.M.L.

3 On 1 Sept. 1587 Roger May, yeoman, appeared at the city Quarter Sessions on two charges of brutal assault on one Peter Waite (YCA, F5, f. 49v). His brother bequeathed him his long black cloak and a bond for what was possibly a bad debt; he restricted his executorship powers to that bond.

4 In 1597, their father, probably retired, was living in the hamlet of Denmead in the parish of Hambledon. (BIHR: CP. G3054, 3111, Cause Papers in May *contra* May, 1599. Henry May had bequeathed a small sum to his father, of the same name, who died the following year, bequeathing this legacy, still unpaid, to his second wife and her children. The widow of the former Lord Mayor of York kept back the money until the date of her father-in-law's death was proved.)

5 Henry May must have been comparatively young, for although he lived until 1596, his father outlived him. See n. 4 above.

6 See n. 2 above. Henry May became a chamberlain in 1568, not 1567.

7 BIHR: Wills 26, ff. 382v–384r.

8 YCA: QS Bk F4, f. 129v.

9 'Henry May, alderman, mayor, and Anne Thomson were married the xvth day of February' 1585/6 (BIHR: Parish register of St Martin Coney St.).

10 *True Report*, unpublished portion (MS. A, f. 68v).

11 BIHR: PR. Y/MCS 17 (Churchwardens' accounts of St Martin Coney St., vol. 2): 'Received of Lady May for the erecting of Mr Drawswerd his Tomb: wherein she caused his daughter Maud to be buried ij s.' (f. 7v); 'To erecting Mr Drawswerd his Tomb in the Churchyard ij s.

iij d.' (f. 11r) (1588–9). The wife of a Lord Mayor of York bore the title 'Lady' for the rest of her life. Drawswerde, who died in 1529, had been a considerable benefactor to St Martin's parish, hoping to found a chantry there. His daughter Maud received a large bequest from him, in reversion. The only woman of her Christian name buried at St Martin's between 1570 and 1589 was Maud Abbot, on 7 Dec. 1587. T. Drawswerde's will is printed in SS lxxix, 267–8.

12 In 1524 Drawswerde granted to the city Corporation all his interest in Holtby Hall in Davygate (YCA: Ho. Bk B10, f. 76). In 1535 when two properties on the south-west side of Davygate were given to the Vicars Choral, the boundaries of both included land formerly belonging to Thomas Drawswerde (YML: Vicars Choral archives, Vo 65). His will refers to properties in the parishes of St Helen and St Martin, among others. The second marriage of Lady Anne May was to a member of the Thwaites family, who also owned premises in Davygate.

13 As n. 10 above.

IV

1 Two original decrees of the Council, dated 16 May 1572 and 22 April 1573, found among the Vicars Choral archives in YML.

2 'I pass not' means, 'I care not'. (Margaret Clitherow was to use this expression at a crucial moment.)

3 C. J. D. Ingledew, *Ballads and songs of Yorkshire* (1860), 117.

V

1 Westminster Cathedral Archives 28, no. 38. (I owe this reference to the kindness of Fr Godfrey Anstruther, O.P. K.M.L.)

2 YAS rec. ser. xlv, 17.

3 BIHR: Wills 17, f. 394v.

4 Often recorded as 'Edward'.

5 He was certainly still living in 1611, and probably in 1614.

6 The house of John Clitherow was divided into two by 1731, and the fronts have been rebuilt in brick; it is now nos. 10–11 Shambles. (No. 10 Shambles was formerly occupied by the sculptor Robert Brumby, who fired his statue of the Madonna and Child (now in the Metropolitan Cathedral of Christ the King, Liverpool) in St Margaret's house, unaware of its identity.) See my article, 'Three sites in the city of York' (in *Rec. Hist.*, xii, no.1, Jan.1973). A detailed account of the research leading to this identification has been deposited in YPL. K.M.L.

7 BIHR: CP. G2011, 2026, 2035, 2103, 2112, 2115, 2116, 2987; H187,

229, 259, 277, 379. Several of these papers have been published in YAS rec. ser. cxiv.

8 It is suggested, rather tentatively, that his estate may have been more or less identical with that of Cornbrough and Brownmoor Farms as sold in June 1917. (Sale particulars in YPL.)

9 As late as 1851 there were slaughter-houses behind some of the Shambles properties (*VCH York*, 283).

VI

1 BIHR: HCAB3, f. 131v.

2 BIHR: D/C CP. 1541/4.

3 BIHR: HCAB6, f. 180r.

4 J. S. Purvis, *Tudor parish documents*, 166–7.

5 A. Stacpoole, *The noble city of York*, 685, n. 12. 'In itself the Bull was irregular and indefensible from the point of view of canon law; it condemned Elizabeth for taking the title of Supreme Head, which she had expressly refused.' (A. L. Rowse, *The England of Elizabeth*, 494, referring to A. O. Meyer, *England and the Catholic Church under Queen Elizabeth*, 82–3.)

6 1619 *Abstract*. (See App. I.)

7 *Cal. S.P. Dom. Eliz. Add. 1566–79*, 224.

8 P. Caraman, *The other face*, 200.

9 E. I. Watkin, *Roman Catholicism in England from the Reformation to 1950*, 29.

10 J. C. H. Aveling, *Catholic recusancy in the city of York, 1558–1791*, 41.

11 YCA: Ho. Bk B27, ff. 112v–113v.

12 BIHR: Wills 22, ff. 638v–639r. When Jane Blenkarne, daughter to Mr Thomas Blenkarne (and Katherine his wife) was baptized at St Michael le Belfrey church on 9 June 1583, her godfather was Mr Blackaller (the Lord President's servant), and godmothers, Mrs Turner *alias* Fale (widow of Edward Turner) and Mrs Jackson, wife of Thomas Jackson (and successor to Margaret Clitherow's cousin Anne). (BIHR: Register of St Michael le Belfrey.)

VII

1 J. C. H. Aveling, *York*, 184.

2 J. Morris, *The troubles of our Catholic forefathers*, iii. 252.

3 BIHR: HCAB9, f. 94v. All members of the Council in the North were also Ecclesiastical Commissioners, and certain members of the city Corporation were from time to time added to their number.

4 Aveling, op. cit., 177–82.

5 J. S. Purvis, *Tudor parish documents*, 166, 67 (Tesimond); CRS xxii, 20 (Tesimond, Oldcorne); Morris, op. cit., 302, 317, 254 (Oldcorne, Godfrey). William Tesimond was the father of Oswald Tesimond, a Jesuit priest; Thomas Oldcorne must have been related to Edward Oldcorne, also a Jesuit priest, whose father, John, was a York brick-layer. Both Oswald Tesimond and Edward Oldcorne were to be variously involved in the 'Gunpowder Plot'; Tesimond escaped, but Oldcorne was executed at Worcester in 1606.

6 BIHR: HCAB9, f. 165r. On 13 April 1583 the High Commission, considering John Clitherow's poor estate, decreed that he should pay only 40s. after forfeiting a recognizance for £40 (HCAB10, f. 199v).

7 Aveling, op. cit., 194.

8 id., 196.

9 BIHR: HCAB10, ff. 28r–v, 88v–89r.

10 P. Hughes, *The Reformation in England*, iii, 429.

11 H. Foley, S.J., *Records of the English Province of the Society of Jesus*, iii (1878), 204, 256–7.

VIII

1 YML: Dean & Chapter archives, E3 (Fabric rolls).

2 BIHR: Administration of the goods of Mary Clitherow, granted 15 Nov. 1572 to Edmund Clitherow her brother, William Calvert, and Millicent Calvert *alias* Clitherow, her sister (Probate Act Book, City); Probate of will of William Calvert of York, butcher, granted to relict Millicent and son John (two other childern mentioned), 20 Nov. 1603 (Wills 29, f. 195).

3 J. C. H. Aveling, *York*, 193–4. See also chap. XVII.

4 BIHR: HCAB10, f. 69.

5 *YCR*, vii, 174.

6 Great play was made with Campion's 'confessions', the government wishing to discredit him publicly in every way they could. On the scaffold, Campion 'asked forgiveness of any whose names he might have compromised during his examination'. But, as Evelyn Waugh has pointed out, the examiners were already well informed from other sources. At the beginning of his Conferences with the Anglican clergy, Campion was questioned, in the presence of the examiners themselves, about his treatment on the rack, but when he provocatively gave them an opportunity to accuse him of betraying his brethren, the question was immediately dropped, that he might not challenge the 'confessions' being circulated under his name. (See E. Waugh, *Edmund Campion* (3rd edn., 1961), 159–67, 196.)

7 *Acts of the Privy Council*, new ser. xiii (1896), 152–3.

8 J. Morris, *Troubles*, iii, 312.

9 P. Caraman, *The other face*, 200 (from Fr Grene's *Collectanea*).

IX

1 YCA: QS Bk F3 (8 March 25 Eliz.).
2 id. (3 Aug. 24 Eliz.).
3 The Council met four times a year in General Sessions, and then as a criminal court; its Commissions of Oyer and Terminer and Gaol Delivery empowered it to try cases of treason, murder and felony. (R. R. Reid, *The King's Council in the North*, 276–7, 283–6; F. W. Brooks, *The Council of the North*, 19.)
4 P. McGrath, *Brasenose priests and martyrs under Elizabeth I* [1985], 9–11 (p. 16, portrait; p. 20, photo. of relic of hand, now with the Poor Clares of Arundel); P. Caraman, *The other face*, 210.

X

1 A. Stacpoole, *York*, 692, n. 23.
2 J. C. H. Aveling, *York*, 71. John Mush was made deacon in the chapel of the English College, Rome, on 5 March 1581, but the date of his ordination to the priesthood is not known (G. Anstruther, *The seminary priests*, i, 240). In Sept. 1583, Mush and three others, 'all in priests' orders', kissed the Pope's foot and left for England (H. Foley, *Records*, vi (1880), 100).
3 The name 'Margaret' is derived from the Greek word for 'a pearl'.
4 Dogmatic decrees of the Council of Trent, Session 22, Chap. 6 (H. B. Coxon, *Roman Catholicism* (1911), 37).
5 This Old English term for Vespers occurs as early as the eleventh century.
6 In 1581 John Clitherow was sued by the farmer of the tithes of Sutton-on-the-Forest for refusing to pay tithe wool and lambs from his flock of 200 sheep pasturing on that part of his Cornbrough estate that lay in the parish of Sutton. The aged vicar stated that by local custom Clitherow should not have pastured his sheep in Sutton at all, because he was only occasionally resident. The case continued in 1582; the result is not known, but the evidence tends to contradict Clitherow's position. In 1583 the farmer of the tithes of Whitwell sued him for tithe wool and lambs on his flock of 200 sheep pasturing on lands formerly belonging to Kirkham Priory; John Clitherow claimed that these lands had been parcel of the priory's demesne land, on which no tithe was payable. The Final Sentence in this case, dated 21 Nov. 1583, survives: the verdict went against him. He was sued again in 1597. He was still refusing to

pay tithe on sheep pastured in Whitwell (where he occupied nine closes) in 1605–7. (For references, see n. 7 to chap. V above.)

XI

1 Margaret has been criticized for this action, but if Henry inherited her spirit, he would think it all a tremendous adventure. He was approaching the age when he would be subject to the penal laws against recusants; Margaret ensured that he would be steadily educated in a much safer environment than was possible in England.

2 YML: Chapter Act Book, 1565-1634, f. 221v.

3 YCA: QS Bk F3 (4 Oct. 23 Eliz.).

4 Blenkarne had been made free as recently as 25 Jan, 1587 (as an 'innholder'); half the fee due had been returned to him for 'good causes' apparent to the Lord Mayor (Henry May) and Aldermen (YCA: Ho. Bk B29, f. 166).

5 J. Morris, *Troubles*, iii, 137 (Fr Richard Holtby, S.J., writing *c.* 1593-5).

6 Margaret would, of course, have been unable to attend the funeral. Depression after her mother's death is likely to have increased her desire to leave York.

7 In 1577 John Dineley, Lord Mayor, had been lectured by the High Commission on his position as 'a man who is set to govern a city and cannot govern his own household'; he had a recusant wife. (J. C. H. Aveling, *York*, 176.)

8 YCA: Ho. Bk B29, f. 125. The words in italics were deleted from the record at a later date (probably in 1609, when the Earl Marshal ruled that the action was incorrect), but they are still legible, and the marginal note remains.

9 id., B29, f. 123.

10 id., B27, f. 266v.

11 In the Parliament of 1584–5 attempts to disbar James VI of Scotland from succeeding to the throne of England in the event of a successful assassination attempt by his mother's supporters upon the life of Queen Elizabeth, were foiled by the Queen herself. (Sir J. E. Neale, *Elizabeth I and her Parliaments, 1584–1601*, 33–6, 52–3).

XII

1 YCA: Ho. Bk B27, ff. 223v, 225.

2 BIHR: Wills 27, ff. 432v–434r (R. Man, 1598).

3 BIHR: Wills 21, ff. 416r–417v (E. Turner, 1580).

4 This appears to be the correct reading; it is found in MSS. [B], C, and the important G, also in the 1619 *Abstract*. See App. I below.

5 YCA: Ho. Bk B28, f. 5.
6 YCA: QS Bk F4, f. 181v.
7 BIHR: HCAB10, ff. 217r, 229(a)v.
8 BIHR: Wills 23, f. 616v (William Tesimond, 14 Nov. 1587). This will has a Calvinistic preamble, probably dictated by William Fothergill, notary public (frequently scribe to the High Commission), the first witness named. However, the register copy contains a memorandum 'that after making this will, William Tesimond by word of mouth made Oswald Tesimond his son co-executor'; the witnesses to this were the remaining two who had witnessed the written will. Tesimond had deliberately waited until Fothergill left, for Oswald was one of the two sons he had sent abroad for Catholic education (he mentions a second, James, in his written will, in guarded terms); he became a Jesuit priest. To be 'co-executor' with his mother and youngest brother was impossible for Oswald; surely his father was *begging for Masses?*

XIII

1 J. C. H. Aveling (*York*, 6) is incorrect in stating that the Guildhall was used only for meetings of the Common Council and a few municipal courts. Contemporary references in the York House Books show that the Assizes for the city were indeed held there, e.g. George Kitchinge bought a house next to the place in the Common Hall where the prisoners were kept at the Assizes (B28, Jan. 1585); George Kitchinge is to have a little house on the north of the Common Hall and to permit the sheriffs and their officers and others to have such easement etc. therein at all Assizes as has been accustomed (B31, 9 Feb. 1593). (I owe these references to Mrs. R. J. Freedman, City Archivist. K.M.L.) The Earl of Huntingdon built another Hall in the Castle Yard, where the Assizes for the county were held; this also was called 'the Common Hall' (J. Morris, *Troubles*, iii, 80; *VCH York*, 525).
2 The Lord President was in poor health at this time; the 'Yorkshire Recusant' (probably John Mush) says in 1586 that he is seldom on the bench now to condemn (Morris, op, cit., 81). The Vice-President was able to exercise all his powers (R. R. Reid, *The King's Council in the North*, 247). Lord Evers (or Eure) may have remembered Margaret from the time when she lived in St Martin's parish; he had lived there himself from at least 1570 (BIHR: PR. Y/MCS F3).
3 John Clench, Baron of the Exchequer 1581; Justice of the Queen's Bench 1584; first Recorder of Ipswich; monument in Holbrook Church, Suffolk.
4 Francis Rodes, one of the salaried, legal members of the Council in the North 1574-85; Justice of the Common Pleas 1585; still a Councillor. From Derbyshire; in 1583 he began to build a large house at

Barlborough, two miles from the Yorkshire boundary. By statute, no
man of law was to be a judge of Assize in the county of his birth or
residence; Rodes defied the spirit of the law by building up extensive
estates in South Yorkshire.

5 In the whole of the northern circuit, the area of the Council's jurisdiction, the Assize judges were associated in this way with the Council in
the North. The Councillors, who did not invariably follow common
law practice, were able to examine both the defendant and the witnesses before a case came before them for trial.

6 As Justices of the Peace, aldermen were expected to attend throughout
the Assizes, for their own education in the law.

7 J. S. Cockburn, *A history of English assizes*, 117.

8 A list of Causes of Death was compiled; the entry for Margaret
Clitherow read, '*ob receptum hospitio Franciscum Inglebaeum*' (C. A.
Newdigate, S.J., 'Quelques notes sur les catalogues des martyrs
anglais dits de Chalcédoine et de Paris', in *Analecta Bollandiana*, lvi
(1938), 308–33).

9 CRS v, 365.

10 I can only guess that the date of the discovery of signs of occupation
and church 'stuff' in a secret room adjacent to Margaret's house was
taken as the date of the 'harbouring'; the wording of an indictment had
to be specific. K.M.L.

11 Probably women had to remove their hats to enable witnesses to
identify defendants with greater certainty; men removed them from
respect.

12 The judge was perhaps over-optimistic. In 1616 at Leicester, nine
women were to be condemned for witchcraft on the evidence of a single
boy (Cockburn, op. cit., 120).

13 Morris, op. cit., 85.

14 E. E. Reynolds, *The trial of St Thomas More* (1964), 121.

15 YCA: QS Bks (F): 12 Oct. 1582 (William Calvert); 11 Jan. 1583, 20
Nov. 1587 (George Middleton).

16 Cockburn, op. cit., 111, 113, 116, 119, 123.

17 H. Hallam, *The constitutional history of England*, i (1908), 231. 'There is
no room for wonder at any verdict that could be returned by a jury,
when we consider what means the government possessed of securing it.
The sheriff returned a panel, either according to express directions, of
which we have proofs, or to what he judged himself of the crown's
intention and interest' (id., 233). (This work was first published in
1827.) An illuminating account of the even more outrageous proceedings in a Gaol Delivery in November 1596, conducted only by the
Council in the North, is given in a letter from the chief participant,
Edward Stanhope, one of the legal members of the Council, to his
brother (BL Addit. MSS. 30,262.E.2). As senior judge on duty, he
gave the charge and managed the Sessions, the most important busi-

ness being the trial of six Catholics framed for attempting a conversion. He chose special grand juries, 'and juries for life [*sic*], such as were sound in religion themselves, and their kin'. All the defendants (Anne Tesh and her companions) were found guilty of high treason, and Stanhope himself 'gave judgement of them', the men to be hanged, drawn and quartered, and the women to be burned.

18 Richard Verstegan, *Theatrum crudelitatum haereticorum nostri temporis*, 76: '*Et cum ex voluntate eorum respondere nollet, nec quenquam nominare (ne alicui mortis esset causa, neve in tantas cruciatuum miserias traheret, ac naufragii in fide occasionem daret) morti admodum crudeli adiudicata est . . .*' This account is taken from Fr John Bridgewater, S.J., *Concertatio ecclesiae catholicae in Anglia . . .* Treves, 1588. (I have not used Verstegan's account of the martyrdom, which was followed by Challoner, because it is notoriously inaccurate on one point, and its ultimate source is not known. K.M.L.)

19 i.e. settle her case. The word does not necessarily connote 'by death'.

20 *Peine forte et dure*, pressing to death, was not, strictly speaking, a sentence but a sanction, originally an attempt to force the defendant who stood 'mute of malice' to plead. The word 'sentence' does appear to have been used by the judge, but in the 16th and early 17th centuries it could be used in a less technical sense of 'judgement' or 'decision', e.g. Acts 15.19 (A.V.). It has seemed simpler to keep the word in some places in my text for the sake of intelligibility. K.M.L.

XIV

1 The case of Grace Claxton (see chap. XVII) shows that the plea for the 'benefit of the *venter*' had to be made by the defendant in answer to the question, 'Have you anything to say why judgement should not be passed upon you?' In Margaret's case, as there had been no trial, there could be no judgement, and the question was not asked. The judge's unlegalistic remarks reveal how far he was prepared to go to save Margaret.

2 Ralph Hurlestone was a fanatical Puritan who, with Huntingdon as his patron, entered Parliament later in 1586 solely to promote his extreme views on church government, and was sent to the Tower with Peter Wentworth and others of his circle. (P. W. Hasler (ed.), *The House of Commons, 1558–1603* (History of Parliament Trust, 1981), ii, 355–6.)

3 The judge's predicament was that had he passed a sentence after trial, he would have had power to grant a reprieve; but *peine forte et dure* was a sanction, intended originally to force the defendant to plead, but by long tradition continued until death intervened. Only the royal prerogative of mercy could deal with the anomalous situation into which Margaret's refusal to stand trial had led her, but the Council in the North was a

prerogative court, and within its area the Lord President (or in his absence the Vice-President) exercised, in a manner probably defined rather vaguely, the royal prerogative. That was why the judge 'referred all to the Council'. (This situation did not arise with the few priests who refused to plead, for they were charged with treason, and the law reserved *peine forte et dure* for cases of felony. Defendants standing mute on treason charges were recorded as pleading Guilty.)

4 From this point onwards, the writer of MS. G (see App. I below) refers to Margaret as 'the martyr'; previously she has been 'the wife', 'the woman', 'the mistress', 'the prisoner', 'she'. It was even harder to bear solitary witness and to resist the natural desire for life in the circumstances of her final imprisonment than in the dramatic surroundings of a law court.

5 The words 'on his death-bed' have been dropped from MS. A; they confirm the date of Fr Comberford's death, which has been uncertain.

6 James Cottrell was a member of a significant Protestant group; one of his godsons was the son of Paul Wood (BIHR: Wills 26, ff. 165v–167r, Cottrell, 1595), who was appointed supervisor to the wills of Henry May (id., ff. 382v–384r, 1596) and of Thomas Blenkarne (id., Wills 31, f. 767r, 1611), husband of Margaret Clitherow's cousin Katherine Turner.

7 He is reported as standing up to intervene in the court; if he had been allowed a seat, had he perhaps served as chaplain to the Assize court? That might account for his visits to Margaret.

8 Wigginton concedes that Catholics are dying for religion, not for treason.

9 Henry May's accusations amounted to a savage and venomous attack upon Margaret's reputation; they have been published, with Fr Mush's comments (from MS. A) in *AJ*, Summer 1971, 29–31.

XV

1 So, too, the Anglican King Charles 'the Martyr', on waking on his execution day, said, ' "Herbert, this is my second marriage-day; I would be as trim today as may be; for before night I hope to be espoused to my blessed Jesus." He then appointed what clothes he would wear . . .' (Sir Thomas Herbert, *Memoirs of the two last years of the reign of King Charles I* (1839), 184).

2 The precise details of what Margaret did with the tapes are uncertain; that she sewed them to the sleeves of her 'habit' is the present writer's interpretation. There is no doubt whatever that she 'prepared', 'provided' or 'ordained' the 'inkle strings' to bind her hands, and that they were so used (although the sheriffs should have provided cords). At an early stage in the transmission of the MS. a line was dropped, so that

[B], C, D and G describe Margaret as leaving the prison 'having trimmed up her head with new inkle strings, which she had prepared to bind her hands'. This struck the editor of the 1619 *Abstract* as so painfully ludicrous that he implies that she carried the inkle strings over her arm with the 'habit', and 'her headgear was decently put on'. MSS. A and F, and the summary in Fr Grene's *Collectanea*, with slight variations, read, 'having trimmed up her head with new inkle and carrying on her arm the new habit of linen with inkle strings. . . .' See App. I below.

3 Or else in one of the Kidcotes next door. It is clear that during the day supervision by the gaoler was slack and prisoners in the two Kidcotes had easy access to the New Counter; periodically the regulations were tightened up.

4 *sic* MSS. D and G, and the 1619 *Abstract*. See App. I below.

XVI

1 Margaret's reply to one of the many charges that she died not for religion but for maintaining traitors in her house, was, 'I deny it, I kept no traitors; make of it what you will, I pass not. I take witness I die for the Catholic faith, the same that I was christened in.'

XVII

1 BL, Addit. MSS. 30,262.E.2.
2 YCA: QS Bk F5, f. 151r.
3 CRS v, 239.
4 P. Caraman, *The other face*, 198.
5 *John Gerard: the autobiography of an Elizabethan;* transl. by P. Caraman (1951), 53.
6 MS. F. See App. I below.
7 The whole passage was published in *AJ*, Summer 1971, 24 n.4. The present writer, being convinced for reasons of topography and history that the route taken would have been that from Micklegate Bar, and having given much thought to the contemporary circumstances over a wide area, found a spot containing a small late sixteenth-century vault constructed beneath a former chantry chapel belonging to a staunchly recusant family. This vault had been excavated in 1917, but its origin was still unknown. The presence of a cobbled floor showed that inhumation was not at first intended, but the depositing of sealed coffins. (Inhumation had been practised at a later date, for human bones were found in a shallow layer of earth.) The head of the family

concerned had been outlawed for high treason in 1716, and the forfeiture of the property to the Crown would sufficiently account for the removal of a martyr's body, supposing that it had been placed there. St Margaret's body, wherever it may be, rests in safety.

8   B. Camm, O.S.B., *Forgotten shrines* (1910), 370.

9   J. Morris, *Troubles*, iii, 317. One of the sheriffs responsible for this inhumane action was John Clitherow's cousin, John Weddell. James Mudd, John Clitherow's brother-in-law, was sheriff the following year; St Margaret's death had restored the whole family to favour.

10 YCA: Ho. Bk B31, f. 20.

11 A. Hamilton, O.S.B. (ed.),   *The chronicle of the English Augustinian Canonesses Regular of the Lateran, at St Monica's in Louvain* . . . [v.1] (1904), 33–4, 120.

12 T. F. Knox (ed.), *The First and Second Diaries of the English College, Douay* . . . (1878), 222; BL, Harleian MS. 296, f. 3r; CRS xxxvii, 74.

13 CRS liv, 126.

14 BIHR: Wills 26, ff. 382v–384r.

15 BIHR: HCAB14, f. 31v ; Wills (original), 1636.

16 G. Anstruther, *The seminary priests*, i, 332. Stapleton may have been the source of the information in Bridgewater/Verstegan; Margaret had 'harboured' him too, and did not betray him.

17 BIHR: Parish registers of St Martin, Coney St.

18 *The Parliamentary* . . . *history of England*, vii (1751), 287–8.

19 G.E.C., *The complete peerage* (new rev. edn., 1910–59), heading Eure.

20 Burke, *Extinct and dormant baronetcies*, 449; J. Foster, *Pedigrees of the county families of Yorkshire*, iii, North and East Riding (1874), Pedigree of Constable of Flamborough, etc.

G.E.C., *Complete peerage*, heading Langdale, gives the mother of Lennox Rodes not as Frances but Catherine, confusing her, apparently, with her own mother, Catherine, daughter of John Holme of Paull Holme, who married (1) Marmaduke Constable, (2) John Moore of York. (In the registers of St Michael le Belfrey, Frances Constable appears as 'daughter to Mr More, lawyer', i.e. step-daughter.)

21 MS. A, f. 84r (unpublished).

Appendix I

Fr John Mush's *True Report* and its History

This work is known from internal evidence to have been completed before 3 June 1586, when Fr Francis Ingleby was executed (Morris, *Troubles*, iii, 358). The earliest external evidence of its existence is found in the 'notes' compiled by William Hutton, a draper, of Christ Church parish, recusant, prisoner in Ousebridge Kidcote, dated 10 December 1594 (id., 301), which refer to an event which had taken place about eight years previously, *c.* 1586–7. A certain Thomas Harwood, gentleman, recusant, imprisoned since 1580, 'being accused by one Pennington, who was in the same prison for debt, for writing of Mrs Clitherow's book of her life, and arraignment at the bar before the judges', was summoned before the Council, and not long afterwards died in the low prison in the Castle.

Fr Mush, author of the account of St Margaret's life, the introductory chapter and the final, very long tirade against her 'murtherers', much of which remains unpublished (some portions were published in *Ampleforth Journal*, Summer 1971, 29–31), claims for the important chapters on her arrest, arraignment, examinations in prison, and martyrdom, to 'report no more than that which I have received from the mouths of divers honest and credible persons, which were present witnesses and beholders of every action'. This can hardly be true in every particular, for a hunted priest had to be very careful of his company; Mrs. Yoward, even Mrs Vavasour, or William Hutton's wife, Mary, also in prison, are unlikely to have spoken to him directly, let alone the person who overheard, or heard about, the judges' private conversations after Margaret's condemnation. The basic editing may have been done by William Hutton himself, for prison life was often curiously free by modern standards, Hutton certainly wrote a good deal, including Mrs Vavasour's letters, and his 'Notes' have exactly the limpid, detached and literary style that marks these chapters of the *True Report*. (His notes actually contain a précis of the material, slightly garbled, as though written down later from memory (Morris, 308–310).)

As for those 'honest and credible persons', the oral sources of the narrative, we can now begin to glimpse them. York society was never fully polarized into Catholic and Protestant, and the nine-days'-wonder of Margaret's acceptance of so appalling a death must have been freely discussed everywhere. Thomas Jackson, who had married her cousin-german, was still alive, practising as an attorney before the Council, on the verge of becoming an alderman, with contacts over a wide area among both professional and business people; he had very strong motives for being present in court himself, and is likely to have picked up the gist of the judges' conversation, in the haunts of the York lawyers, or even to have been present at them in some capacity. There may have been other such officials, not yet traced, with a personal as well as a professional interest in the circumstances of Margaret's death.

The following letters were used to distinguish the surviving manuscripts of the *True Report* in Appendix I of *Margaret Clitherow* (which should be consulted for further details):

A. Late 16th-century, published by Fr Morris in *Troubles*, iii (1877), but not in its entirety, nor with complete accuracy; it was, I believe, transcribed by another person on behalf of Fr Morris. The 16th-century copyist being imperfectly acquainted with English orthography, the text is in fact very corrupt. No title-page survives; the heading reads: 'A trewe reporte of the li[fe]/and marterdome of Mrs / Margarete Clitherowe'. Part of folios 1, 86–7 have been lost since Fr Morris published them. (Formerly in the possession of the Middelton family, and now the property of the R. C. diocese of Middlesbrough; kept at York Minster Library.) See App. II.

B. Transcript made in 1654. (Bar Convent, York.) Published with alterations and omissions, by W. Nicholson in 1849. Nicholson's statements about his 'faithful transcript' are most confusing, and his erroneous remark that 'the original of the present manuscript is in the possession of . . . Peter Middelton, Esq.', meaning, apparently, that B was copied from A, misled me into thinking that Mr Middelton might have possessed a second MS. Nicholson nowhere states that the Bar Convent MS. is his source; we owe this information to Fr Morris (*Troubles*, iii, 357–8).

C. Transcript made in 1740; bookplate of William Constable, Esq., F.R.S., F.A.S. (of Burton Constable, 1721–91); Lot 31 in Sale Catalogue of Burton Constable MSS, 24 June 1889. (Constable of Everingham MSS., formerly deposited in the East Riding County Record Office, Beverley; now in the Brynmor Jones Library, University of Hull). Almost identical with B, from which it was evidently copied.

D. 16th-century copy of the chapters relating to Margaret's arrest, arraignment, etc. and death (St Mary's College, Oscott; in the Peter Mowle collection of MSS., *complete by 1595*). Evidently copied from G, but 'improved' a trifle here and there.

E. Transcript in a late 18th- or early 19th-century hand, formerly among the Alban Butler MSS. at Archbishop's House, Birmingham, but missing in 1964.

F. Early 17th-century. (Vatican Library, Barberini Latini, Codex 3555.) 2 folios missing. This MS. appears to follow the D recension, even dropping a line dropped in D, but at a few points follows the G recension; it has been edited and slightly abridged, as though for publication.

G. 16th-century copy of chapters dealing with the arrest, arraignment etc. and death only; evidently the original of D. Since a terminal date can be given to D, G must be the earliest surviving copy of these chapters. The work of an extremely careful copyist, who has made very few slips; his spelling is comparatively modern. (York Minster Library, Add. MS. 151.) The portion relating to St. Margaret's arraignment was published by me in *Ampleforth Journal*, Autumn 1970, 350–5.

(*Note*. I have made transcripts of all the MSS. except B; my work is intended to find a permanent home at Ampleforth Abbey. K.M.L.)

An abstract of an English MS. in 12 quarto leaves, in Fr. Christopher Grene's *Collectanea* G (now lost) is included in his *Collectanea* M, now at Stonyhurst. (Fr Grene flourished in the second half of the 17th c.)

Publications

1619 An Abstracte / of the life / and martirdome / of Mistres / Margaret Clitherowe, / who suffered in the yeare of our Lorde / 1586, the 25. of March / At Mackline, / Printed by Henry Iaey An 1619
(Facsimile published in *English Recusant Literature*, vol. 393. Scolar Press, 1979; made from a copy in the library of St Augustine's Priory, Newton Abbot.)

1849 *Life and death of Mrs Margaret Clitherow*, now first published from the original manuscript, and edited by William Nicholson. (1849)
(Actually transcribed from B; the editor has confessedly toned down certain expressions.) This work has as frontispiece the well-known 'portrait' of Margaret Clitherow, which has, however, no claim to authenticity.

1877 'A True report of the life and martyrdom of Mrs Margaret Clitherow'. (In J. Morris, S.J., *The troubles of our Catholic forefathers*, 3rd ser. 1877, reprinted 1970). See App. II.

1970 See note on MS. G, above.

Appendix II
Sources

My main source was originally *The troubles of our Catholic forefathers, related by themselves*, 3rd ser., ed. by J. Morris, S.J., 1877 (reprinted by Gregg International Publishers Ltd. 1970). In order to reduce notes to the minimum, I have omitted, with a few exceptions, all references to this work, which contains contemporary accounts of the persecution in the north of England, and also the results of Fr Morris's researches. Pages 360-440 contain his transcript of Fr Mush's *True Report*. (See Appendix I.)

Since 1966 I have used the archive sources in York extensively; where no reference is given for information relating to conditions in the city in the sixteenth century, it is usually derived from the House Books (York City Archives, class B), either the originals or the extracts printed in *York civic records*, v. 1–9, published in the Yorkshire Archaeological Society's Record Series, 1939–78.

In quoting from the *True Report*, I have usually followed MS. A as printed by Fr Morris, but have occasionally used an obviously more accurate reading from one of the other MSS., acknowledging only the more important changes.

A. Manuscripts
(See also Appendix I.)

All the records of the Council in the North, which would throw so much light on the history of northern recusancy, are missing, save for a very few scraps discovered as 'strays' among other archive groups.

Much genealogical information is to be found in three MS. volumes in York Central Public Library, compiled by R. H. Skaife and entitled *Civic officials of York and Parliamentary representatives*. (This work is, however, not invariably accurate.)

YORK CITY ARCHIVES:

York Corporation House Books.

York and Ainsty Quarter Sessions Books.
Miscellaneous Registers.

BORTHWICK INSTITUTE OF HISTORICAL RESEARCH, YORK:

High Commission Act Books.
Wills.
Parish Registers of St Helen's, Stonegate.
Churchwardens' Accounts of St Martin's, Coney Street.
Cause Papers.

YORK MINSTER LIBRARY:

Vicars Choral archives: Obits.
Dean and Chapter archives: Fabric Rolls, 16th–17th centuries; Fabric Terrier, c.1681–1826; Lease Registers; Chapter Acts, 16th-17th centuries.

B. Printed Works

(Select Bibliography)

Anstruther, G., O.P., *The seminary priests: a dictionary of the secular clergy of England and Wales, 1558–1850*. I. *Elizabethan, 1558–1603*, (1968).

Aveling, H., O.S.B., *The Catholic recusants of the West Riding of Yorkshire, 1558–1790*, 1963.

Aveling, H., O.S.B., *Northern Catholics: the Catholic recusants of the North Riding of Yorkshire. 1558–1790*, 1966.

Aveling, H., O.S.B., *Post Reformation Catholicism in East Yorkshire, 1558–1790*, 1960

Aveling, J. C. H., *Catholic recusancy in the city of York, 1558–1791*, 1970.

Ballam, H., and R. Lewis, *The visitors' book: England and the English as others have seen them, A.D. 1500 to 1950*, 1950.

Benson, G., *An account of the city and county of the city of York from the Reformation to the year 1925*, 1925.

Benson, G., *Later medieval York: The city and county of the city of York from 1100 to 1603*, 1919.

Birt, H. N., O.S.B., *The Elizabethan religious settlement: a study of contemporary documents*, 1907.

Bridgett, T. E., C.S.S.R., and T. F. Knox, *The true story of the Catholic hierarchy deposed by Queen Elizabeth* [1889].

Brooks, F. W., *The Council of the North*, 1953.

Brooks, F. W., *York and the Council of the North*, 1954.

Brunskill, E., *The York Mystery or Corpus Christi Plays*, 1963.

Burton, E. H., and J. H. Pollen, S.J., *Lives of the English martyrs*, 2nd ser., *The martyrs declared Venerable*. v. I, *1583–8*, 1914

Calendars of State Papers, Domestic, Elizabeth.

Camm, B., O.S.B., *Forgotten shrines*, 1910.

Camm, B., O.S.B. (ed.), *Lives of the English martyrs declared Blessed by Pope Leo XIII, in 1886 and 1895*, 2 v., 1904–5.

Caraman, P., S.J. (ed), *The other face; Catholic life under Elizabeth I*, 1960.

Catholic Record Society Publications.

Challoner, R. *Memoirs of missionary priests*, new edn. rev. and corrected by J. H. Pollen, S.J., 1924.

Cockburn, J. S., *A history of English assizes, 1558–1714*, 1972.

Cross, C., 'Priests into ministers: the establishment of Protestant practice in the city of York, 1530–1630' (in P. N. Brooks (ed.), *Reformation principle and practice: essays in honour of Arthur Geoffrey Dickens*, 1980).

Cross, C., *The Puritan Earl: the life of Henry Hastings, third Earl of Huntingdon, 1536–1595*, 1966.

Cross, C., 'The third Earl of Huntingdon and trials of Catholics in the North, 1581–1595' (in *Recusant History*, viii, 1966).

Dickens, A. G., *The English Reformation*, 1964.

Dickens, A. G., 'The first stages of Romanist recusancy in Yorkshire, 1560–1590' (in *Yorkshire Archaeological Journal*, xxxv, 1940–3).

Dickens, A. G., *Lollards and Protestants in the diocese of York, 1509–1558*, 1959.

Dickens, A. G., *The Marian reaction in the diocese of York*, 2 pts., 1957.

Dictionary of National Biography.

Dobson, R. B., 'Admissions to the freedom of the city of York in the late Middle Ages' (in *Economic History Review*, 2nd ser., xxvi, 1973).

Dodds, M. H., and R., *The Pilgrimage of Grace, 1536–1537, and the Exeter conspiracy, 1538*, 2 v., 1915.

Drake, F., *Eboracum; or, the history and antiquities of the city of York*, 1736.

Elton, G. R. (ed.), *The Tudor constitution: documents and commentary*, 1960.

Emmison, F. G., 'The Elizabethan assize files, with particular reference to the county of Essex' (in *Bulletin* of the Society of Local Archivists, xiii, 1954).

Everitt, A., 'The English urban inn, 1560–1760' (in A. Everitt (ed.), *Perspectives in English urban history*, 1973).

Gee, H., *The Elizabethan clergy and the settlement of religion, 1558–1564*, 1898.

Gee, H., and W. J. Hardy, *Documents illustrative of English Church history*, 1896.

Gerard, J., S.J., *John Gerard: the autobiography of an Elizabethan*, transl. by P. Caraman, S.J., 1951.

Gillow. J., *A literary and biographical history, or bibliographical dictionary, of the English Catholics*, 5v.,[1885].

Hallam, H., *The constitutional history of England from the accession of Henry VII to the death of George II*, [1st edn. 1827], 3 v., 1908.

Hasler, P. W. (ed.), *The House of Commons, 1558–1603*, 3v., 1981.

Hughes, P., *The Reformation: A popular history*, 1957.

Hughes, P., *The Reformation in England*, rev. edn., 3 v. in 1, 1963.

Jacob, G., *A new law dictionary*, 1744.

Johnston, A. F., and M. Rogerson, *Records of early English drama: York*, 2 v., 1979.

Knight, C. B., *A history of the city of York*, 1944.

Leys, M. D. R. *Catholics in England, 1559–1829: a social history*, 1961.

Mathew, D., *Catholicism in England: The portrait of a minority, its culture and traditions*, 3rd edn., 1955.

Merrick, M. M., *Thomas Percy, seventh Earl [of Northumberland]*, [1949].

Morris, J., S.J. (ed.), *The troubles of our Catholic forefathers*, 1st ser., 1872.

Neale, Sir J. E., *Elizabeth I and her Parliaments, 1559–1581, 1584–1601*, 2 v., 1953–7.

Neale, Sir J. E., *The Elizabethan House of Commons*, 1949.

Neale, Sir J. E., *Queen Elizabeth*, 1934.

Palliser, D. M., 'A hostile view of Elizabethan York' (in *York Historian*, i, 1976).

Palliser, D. M., *The Reformation in York, 1534–1553*, 1971.

Palliser, D. M., *Tudor York*, 1979.

Palliser, D. M., 'York under the Tudors: the trading life of the northern capital' (in A. Everitt (ed.), *Perspectives in English urban history*, 1973).

Perin, W., O.P., *Spiritual exercises: being ghostly meditations, and a near way to come to perfection and life contemplative* . . . [First pubd. 1557; ed. by C. Kirchberger, 1929], 1957.

Purvis, J. S., *Tudor parish documents of the diocese of York: a selection with introd. and notes*, 1948.

Purvis, J. S., *The York cycle of Mystery Plays: a complete version*, 1957.

Raine, A., *Medieval York: a topographical survey based on original sources*, 1955.

Reid, R. R., *The King's Council in the North*, 1921.

Rowse, A. L., *The England of Elizabeth: the structure of society*, 1950.

[Sharpe, Sir C.] *Memorials of the Rebellion of 1569*, 1840.

Stacpoole, A., O.S.B., and others (eds), *The noble city of York* [1972].

Surtees Society Publications.

Taswell-Langmead, T. P., *English constitutional history*. 10th edn. rev. by T. F. T. Plucknett, 1946.

[Thomas à Kempis] *The Following of Christ*, translated out of Latin into English, A.D. 1556, by Father Richard Whytford, Brigittine of Syon House; ed., with historical introd., by W. Raynal, O.S.B., 1872.

Tierney, M. A. (ed.), *Dodd's Church history of England from the commencement of the sixteenth century to the Revolution in 1688; with notes, additions, and a continuation*, 5 v., 1839–53.

Trimble, W. R., *The Catholic laity in Elizabethan England, 1558–1603*, 1964.

Tyler, P., *The Ecclesiastical Commission and Catholicism in the North, 1562–1577*, Priv. print, Leeds, 1960.

Victoria History of the Counties of England, The City of York, 1961.

Watkin, E. I., *Roman Catholicism in England from the Reformation to 1950*, 1957.

Williams, N., *Thomas Howard, fourth Duke of Norfolk*, 1964.
Yorkshire Archaeological Society Publications.
Yorkshire Parish Register Society Publications.

The version of the mystery plays quoted is that of the late Canon J. S. Purvis, *The York cycle of Mystery Plays* (1957).

Appendix III
Some Notes on Dates

a) *York civic offices (Tudor period)*

The two sheriffs were elected on 21 September and took office on 29 September, Michaelmas Day.

The Lord Mayor was elected on 15 January (St Maur's Day) and took office on 3 February. The chamberlains (the city's treasurers, the number of whom varied from year to year) and the bridgemasters were elected on the same day as the Lord Mayor.

The annual lists of citizens taking out their freedom each year (by apprenticeship, patrimony or payment) were copied into the Freemen's Register under a heading giving the names of the Lord Mayor and chamberlains. This register has been published (Surtees Soc. xcvi, cii) but the editor unfortunately overlooked the difference between the Old and the New Style of dating; the dates in his headlines are slightly more than one year behind the correct date. (The regnal years in his headings do not appear in the original. A safe guide to the date is the mayoralty; the lists given in F. Drake, *Eboracum* are accurate.) Dr. D. M. Palliser first pointed out this error in *Tudor York*, 153, n.2.

(The dates of freemen and chamberlains printed in my *Margaret Clitherow*, pp. 187–93 are consequently incorrect. Their correction has proved of particular significance in speeding up Henry May's rise in the world.)

b) *The Date of the Martydom*

One early list of martyrs gives 26 March 1586 as the date of St Margaret's death, and although Fr Mush gives Friday, 25 March as the day, he creates a little confusion by saying that 'the next day' the ministers attacked her character 'in their pulpits'.

The common sentence of hanging was normally carried out on the Saturday after each Assizes, on the Knavesmire, and became the subject of the ministers' sermons the following day. However, St Margaret had not been sentenced, but condemned to a sanction which was to be inflicted in considerable privacy. The Tollbooth was conveniently close to her prison, and facilities could be provided there; but it was also situated on the route that lay between the Castle (and the Kidcotes) and Micklegate Bar. The condemned criminals were escorted by great crowds along this route, and the sheriffs and parish constables could not have coped with such a mass of the population on the same day as Margaret's death, which itself attracted a great crowd. Hence the Friday was chosen for her execution.

Fr Morris, in 1877, misunderstanding Fr Mush, stated, quite erroneously, 'The day which in England was March 25 by New Style was April 4, and Easter that year falling a week earlier in the New Style than in the Old, that day was Good Friday, N.S.' (*Troubles* iii, 357.) (The present writer absent-mindedly followed Fr Morris in *Margaret Clitherow*.) The statement is an impossibility, for not seven, but ten days had been dropped in 1582; on the continent it was Tuesday.

Another error is found in some of the early lists, which attribute the martyrdom to 1585, the writer being in ignorance of the exact day. In England the New Year still began on 25 March, so St Margaret died on the first day of the year 1586, Old Style.

OUTLINE PEDIGREE of TURNER,

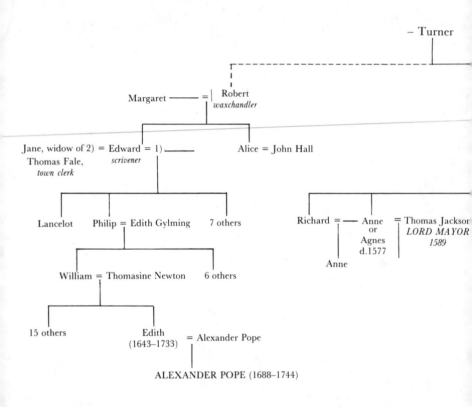

– Turner

Margaret ——— = | Robert
waxchandler

Jane, widow of 2) = Edward = 1) ———   Alice = John Hall
Thomas Fale,   *scrivener*
town clerk

Lancelot   Philip = Edith Gylming   7 others   Richard = —— Anne   = Thomas Jackson
or   *LORD MAYOR*
Agnes   *1589*
d.1577

Anne

William = Thomasine Newton   6 others

15 others   Edith = Alexander Pope
(1643–1733)

ALEXANDER POPE (1688–1744)

MIDDLETON and POPE

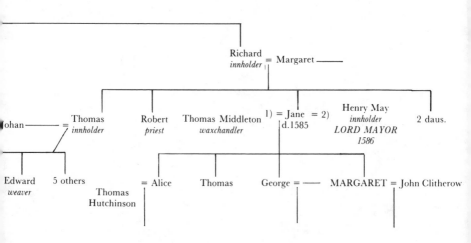